CLIMBING IS THE NEW YOGA

Juan Marbarro

To Gloria and the special light she projects around her.

2022 Juan Marbarro ©
Edition: Fabio Jiménez
Translation: Carmen Lozano
Cover design: Gloria Jiménez

Climbing Letters
climbingletters.com

ISBN: 978-84-123960-4-1
All rights reserved ©

Contents

Introduction 7
Climbing and Yoga 11
Yoga 16
The ego and the mind: the problem 20
The proposal: the 8 steps 25
Yamas 31
Niyamas 43
Recap 55
Asana 58
Pranayama 64
Pratyahara 71
Dharana 75
Dhyana 79
Samadhi 81
Samyama 85
Sadhana 89
Swami Climbananda 98
Glossary 131
Yogic Readings 139

Introduction

Today, yoga and climbing share a common problem: both have been boxed in as a physical practice, reduced to a series of spectacular movements, impressive photographs, a well-built body, being strong and flexible. Or to physical achievements such as sending difficult routes or performing complicated *asanas* (postures). In short, to what feeds the ego: the merely aesthetic, sporting achievements or competition. However, both are much more, or at least have the potential to be if we go deeper in that direction.

In any case, instead of lamenting this situation, we can take it on the bright side and say that, thanks to this "circus", there is a message that is getting through, to a greater or lesser extent, but it is getting through, nonetheless. The truth is many people are starting out with that motivation, but they then discover that there is much more to it. And that much more has immeasurable benefits, as we will see in the rest of the book. Let's say that, initially, our ego is attracted to these phenomena (physical activity or the merely aesthetic), but the truth is that this attraction can actually be a trap for it. As we deepen in these practices, be it climbing or yoga, we have the opportunity to reduce the ego's influence on ourselves. We can dissolve its layers until we achieve greater clarity in our lives. If we manage, of course, to stop the ego from turning against us and blowing up in our face.

It is convenient here to quickly clarify what is understood by ego. One of the definitions I like the most is that the ego is a set of conditionings of the mind with which we identify ourselves and which, in this way, permeate throughout our whole life. It is a bit dense to go into this in the introduction of the book, but it is good to touch base on this here and then go deeper later on.

These conditionings that are the ego are the ones that take away our peace of mind and the serenity necessary to live (or climb) well. These conditionings are the system through which we filter reality (yes to this, no to that, this is good, this is bad, I can or I cannot, etc.). In many cases these conditionings are wrong or are not adapted to the objective situation, so they end up being an obstacle to our development.

Yoga is, then, a path to peace of mind that goes through the dissolution of the various layers of the ego that hinder it. And it is, therefore, a way back home, since this peace of mind —it can also be called happiness— is the natural state of the mind, its purest state, free from the modifications that agitate, disturb and contaminate it.

Through climbing we can also travel this path if we set our minds to it, as I have been arguing in previous books. In this case, I want us to explore the points that these two paths (yoga and climbing) have in common, how yoga and its philosophy can be used in climbing and how we can practice yoga through climbing. Or simply use both to have a deeper knowledge of ourselves.

With these few lines I imagine that you have already realized that this is not so much about postures or how to improve strength or flexibility. This book is mainly oriented to the philosophical-spiritual part of yoga which, being its most important part, is not always accessible (among other things because we get too distracted by the physical practice). The body, its strengthening and the maintenance of health are a part of yoga, yes, but it is part of a much larger system and is subordinate to greater goals. It is like having a tree in the garden and enjoying the good shade it gives. If you ignore that its fruits are edible, very tasty and have many properties, you will be, by ignorance, losing much of what it can offer you. The shade is good, but we would only be enjoying a small part of the tree's potential.

The philosophy of yoga has been studied and transmitted for thousands of years, and there are many texts of different currents. On the other hand, the philosophical part of climbing has been developed in a more personal and intuitive way. Each of the people who have been practicing it and who have felt, in their own way, the spiritual growth and the approach to its essence, have been transmitting it without ever consolidating it as a system or path of spiritual development. It does have its own ethical codes and such, which are a part of any philosophy, but at the moment it is not explicitly established as a spiritual path, although many people walk the path intuitively and benefit from its contributions in our lives. Perhaps it has not been instituted as a spiritual practice because it is a more recent activity, and its effects and benefits are measured through criteria such as those of competition or sports science. In this sense, yoga has thousands more years of experience and refinement.

After all, one of the main differences between a sports practice and a spiritual one is the intention. If your intention is to move up a grade or compete with the next guy, it is a sports practice. If your intention is to know yourself better, grow and improve yourself, it may be a spiritual practice.

Climbing and Yoga

Thousands of people experience the relationship between climbing and yoga intuitively. For some reason, they are attracted to both. In the physical realm it is almost obvious how they complement each other, there is no need to elaborate the argument too much. But from a philosophical point of view or as a path to self-realization they can also complement each other. In this book I want to explore why and how, what these two practices, separated by thousands of years and thousands of kilometers, have in common. In addition, I want to further explore this relationship to make the most of the synergies that can be generated by crossing both paths. Thus, anyone will be able to choose what suits them, as well as gain awareness regarding new possibilities in their practice and the potential effects on their life.

Climbing can be a means of self-knowledge, of self-inquiry, the stage where our lights and shadows manifest themselves. The laboratory where we experiment with ourselves, just as yoga has been doing for thousands of years. Both can —and should— be approached as practical, experiential philosophies. That is, they must be walked and put into practice to know their benefits firsthand, beyond the intellection or assimilation of their concepts. Both yoga and climbing provide the scenarios, the playing field. The screen on which to project our light so that we become aware of our shadows. As a first example of some of the situations that occur in climbing, this light that we project would be our intention to climb a wall. Thanks to the fact that we put ourselves to it we become aware of our fears and limitations. This is the moment in which we gain consciousness of them, the first starting point to overcome them and grow at their expense. As we said, the ego approaches things by appetence and, by doing this, it betrays itself, for these things can ultimately dissolve it.

> Direct your steps toward the wisdom of yoga, for yoga is knowledge in action.
>
> 2.50 Bhagavad Gita[1]

Yoga has been refined over centuries of study and practice to develop precise tools and techniques to help us overcome these obstacles or shadows of the mind. Although today most people think of yoga as a set of stretches, yoga's approach to human development is holistic. It encompasses both body and mind, energies and emotions. It is developed through different paths, not only with stretches on a mat. These are only a small fragment of the practice, although this is the part that has more prominence in today's society.

And here comes the big question: how am I going

---
[1] Translation by Juan Mascaró

to relate yoga and climbing?

Throughout the first part of the book, we will go through the yogic philosophy and explore the possibilities of understanding and using it through climbing. It will be difficult to discern whether we are talking about yogic climbing or whether we are practicing yoga by climbing. Climbing will be used to deepen yoga, as well as yoga to deepen and enhance climbing. In addition, we will look at the impact of both on the life of the practitioner. At some points, this book will cover more practical aspects and at other times climbing may be used as a simile or metaphor to understand some of the yogic concepts. But yes, we can grant this to the ego for now: we will be able to climb better because of yoga and we will also be able to get to the benefits of yoga through climbing.

Since climbing lacks a written philosophical tradition, it will take on the role of a medium, a vehicle through which we will approach the philosophy of yoga. We will understand and use tools and techniques of yoga in climbing, connecting places where both paths cross or could cross, as well as re-knowing in yoga and its different branches the experience of climbing. In the second part of the book, you will find the story of Swami Climbananda, a character that will help to integrate and understand more deeply the essence of climbing understood as a new type of yoga.

It is not an easy task to put these two things

together, but I think you will find many points of support throughout this book. The path of yoga can be difficult but very satisfying. It is a path worth walking, even if its little by little, and every bit of progress counts. Both climbing and yoga can bring enormous effects to your life, in achieving high levels of serenity, peace of mind and happiness. After all, these are the goals of all human activity, even if sometimes we get confused about the path to obtain them.

All philosophies and paths of self-realization have used different tools and ways to achieve the ultimate goal: happiness. In many of them, we can see how these paths coincide or are quite similar, although we are talking about things as apparently different as yoga and climbing. After all, all the rivers run into the sea. When we approach a peak there are several ways to reach it, either by the south or north face, by the ridge or by climbing big walls. But the summit is always the same. Similarly, peace of mind and happiness are the summit to which all wisdoms ultimately aim to rise.

The philosophy of yoga has been transmitted over thousands of years and has come down to our days by various means and from different currents. On many occasions, this wisdom is presented culturally "codified" through Hindu mythologies and mysticisms that make it even more complicated for those who look at it from another culture. Another of the objectives of this book is, precisely, to achieve an approach to yoga through a medium that is familiar to us (climbing), trying to "translate" or rather "interpret" the techniques and tools of yoga to our experience on the rock. Without falling into reductionism and respecting the essence as much as possible. I want to keep this book simple and accessible to everyone, a sort of starting point from which to begin to better understand yoga beyond *asanas* (postures) and climbing beyond going up a wall. Do not be frightened by the presence of Sanskrit terms, as many of them are absolutely essential. To translate them would be to betray them and would limit the understanding of the concepts. Therefore, I will try to respect the terminology and to be as faithful as possible to the real essence of Yoga but leaving as far as possible mysticism and cultural projections that can overshadow the content.

The main idea is to adapt yoga and its philosophy as a frame of reference for inner work in climbing. In yoga, as we will see during this book, the intention is to achieve equanimity, peace of mind above the fluctuations of the mind. If we climb with that intention to achieve being above our thoughts, we can also travel a very interesting and fruitful path in terms of happiness and satisfaction.

Yoga

To see where we are starting from, we must first zoom in a little on what yoga is. The word yoga is commonly translated as "union". It derives from the root "yuj", which means "to bind" or "to unite". It is the same root as "yoke". A yoke is an instrument used to bind two animals together so that they both pull a cart or plow in the same direction. Let's say joining or aligning forces to move a load in the same direction efficiently.

Yoga is, in turn, a yoke that seeks to unite the different parts of your existence. The divided energies (mind and body, negative and positive, good and bad or action and relaxation) are the parts that have been divided throughout life and need to be re-united or aligned to live more fully. We have to eliminate the obstacles and mental conditioning with which we identify ourselves and which divide us and take us away from the true nature that we can find in ourselves. True union is achieved when we integrate all our parts, transcending opposites and putting everything at the service of peace and growth. As in the example of the yoke that binds the animals together, we could say that the yoke unites the laziest ox as well as the most active, the meekest as well as the wildest, so that they all end up pulling in the same direction and at the same pace.

In a way, climbing is also union. The union or alignment of the body with the mind, with the emotions, with nature, the rock, the route and our abilities.

If we say that a yoke serves to chain the forces of animals in the same direction, we find a curious similarity with the term used in Spanish for "sending the route" (when we complete a route in free climbing): encadenar (to chain, chaining, concatenate). It may be related to the fact that the bolt at the end of the route usually has a chain. But, bringing the term down to our purpose, we can think of it as the "chaining" together of all the movements in a precise way to get the route climbed. The union of all the sequences, the union of all our capacities, our forces, our "beasts" (the projections of the mind), toward sending a project (encadenar, chaining). Aligning ourselves with nature (internal and external). Integrate and interconnect the parts as a whole.

Think for a moment about all the conditions that have to be in place for you to be able to send a challenging route: a good attitude, overcoming fears, staying calm, being in good physical condition, identifying and using the most optimal grips or footholds, applying different techniques to position the body in balance, managing energies by squeezing when you have to squeeze and resting when it is necessary or possible, etc. It is something integral and must be balanced. What good would a good physical condition be if we lose our composure as soon as there is a meter and a half between botls? What good is it if we know the grips but do not have the technique to make use of them? What good is it if we are obsessed with the route and squeeze too much without respecting our body and the rests that we could or should use? Of course, all these imbalances are part of the path and show us where we could work to improve, but they do not help us send the route, the master union of all the parts. In this sense, both yoga and climbing can be ways for the unification of dispersed energies, to concentrate our forces, for an efficient use of everything we have at our disposal. A way to overcome the conditioning of the mind that blurs our perception and prevents us from using what is outside its criteria.

> 1.2 Yoga serves to still the movements of the mind.
>
> *Yoga Sutras*, Patanjali

In a way, this is what gets us hooked on the mountain, what makes us want to come back again and again. In the mountain we are in yoga, in union with our nature. It allows us to get out of the loop in which we are continuously immersed in our lives, it allows us to transcend our mental chatter. We are drawn to climbing to the heights to take perspective and distance ourselves from the mental whirlwinds of everyday life. However, we must be attentive. It can also happen that on the mountain we reproduce some of the patterns we want to get out of. By learning about yoga and learning to implement it in climbing we will try to transcend the automatic programming so that the mountain is not just a way to escape. Because if it is, if we don't do the work intentionally, every time we get off the rock our mind will press play again and we will be back in the eye of the hurricane.

To better understand why it is necessary to quiet the mind, the first thing to do is to know the problem. You can't fix something if you don't know what causes it. Even less so if you don't even recognize the existence of the problem at all because you are living within it. I would never fix that weird noise the car engine makes if I thought it was built that way, that it was normal. I will never achieve peace of mind if I think the turmoil and confusion I live in is normal.

The ego and the mind: The problem

You probably know the ego by now. It is the one that lives inside you but is not you. It is the one that limits you, that sabotages your efforts, the one that tells you that you are going to fall in the next step just when you must gather all your strength to be able to take it. It is the one that feels threatened by criticism or growth, by anything that escapes its absolute control. The ego is well-known on the rock: the one who is afraid to fall, the one who is afraid to fail, the one who identifies with the grade it's climbing, the one who does not expose himself beyond what it controls, even if it comes at the cost of slowing down growth or mistreating the body by forcing you to keep climbing. Who is this ego? Where did it come from? Why does it sabotage me? Why does it make itself so apparent in climbing? Is there a button to turn it off? The ego —which will also be called throughout the book the lower self or, simply put, the mind, since the mind is like a container and takes the form of what is projected into it—, the conditionings —yes to this, no to that, this equal to that, etc.—, or the automatisms, whatever we want to call them, are our programming. They are the way in which we are conditioned to execute the same program automatically in everything we do, think and live. A program that permeates all our reality, that conditions all decisions, all results, all the reality of your life. It decides what is real and what is not, what is possible and what is not, what is due and what is not, what is necessary and what is unnecessary. And not only that. It also conditions perceptions. It filters and manipulates what you see, what you hear, what you understand. In short, it impregnates everything it receives with its subjectivity, distorting and manipulating objective reality to make it suit it. With this it pretends that reality never threatens its little world made of illusion (*maya*). It casts its shadows on everything around us and makes us think that this spectacle is reality, when all it does is to focus where it wants to slant the world according to its programming.

And now comes the worst of all: it makes us identify with it. It makes us believe that "we are like that". Or worse, that it is all we are. We have infinite potential and our own mind goes around projecting our limits to such an extent that it totally configures our reality. It reduces it to the size of our learned conditioning. Indeed, learned.

Because, if the situation can get even worse, this is the moment: these conditionings, this ego, this mind, these projections or whatever we want to call them, are imposed from outside, they are learned. They are a concoction of behaviors and patterns that we have been learning throughout life but have been informed from outside.

Since we are born, we accumulate these conditionings that limit our potential. The automatisms that move you through all your life experiences have been programmed by other people. They have been your family, your environment, television; religions, marketing, social networks; your brother-in-law or the neighbor across the street, along with a long etcetera. All these people, with better, worse or no intention, have shaped —and continue to shape— your ego, which is the same that in turn determines your mayavic reality. That is, the illusion that is your life. *Maya* is a term used in yoga and Hinduism to define this illusory reality. *Maya* are the beliefs that create your reality, since they condition all your personal possibilities and, therefore, your decisions. They are all those labels that outline what you think you are and what you think you can be and with which you identify yourself, expanding or limiting your possibilities based on those beliefs. I am a student, I am a lawyer, I am handsome, I am ugly; I am rich, I am poor; I am strong, I am weak; I can travel or I cannot, I belong to this or that nationality, sports team or political party, etc. It is these thousands of more or less absurd ideas that make up this illusion, in most cases shared by several people. And this is what gives a somewhat more solid appearance to the illusion without really being nothing more than projections of the mind.

But, even if they are shared by several people, each one is complicit in it. They have been internalized to the point that you carry them with you everywhere so that you can reproduce them over and over again and try to recreate the same illusion. Even when we understand that reality is changeable and that the only certainty we have is precisely that, that everything is constantly changing. And this is where this ego becomes an obstacle and sabotages us. When something is not within reach of its timeworn tools, it tends to withdraw under any pretext, sabotaging your greatest aspirations so it can keep you inside the fence it has created for you.

Does all this sound familiar to you? Climbing once again presents itself as an ideal terrain in which to recognize this saboteur, this projector of limits and creator of illusory worlds. And these illusory worlds are not part of a virtual metaverse, they are inside you, they are your life. The fears of falling or failing, the frustrations of not meeting your expectations, the aversion to a type of climbing, style, or rock; the little inner voices that make you lose focus at the worst moments, the lack of confidence in your abilities or in the footholds or the grips of your hands. All this and much more are the multiple faces of that ego that we can learn to recognize in ourselves to overcome its shadows and stop creating obstacles, to stop conditioning and creating your reality.

As I said, it is present in all aspects of our life, but

in climbing it becomes quite evident. And we can take the opportunity to grab it the moment it peeks out of the burrow, so that we can do the necessary work of overcoming its projections, illuminating its shadows and dissolving its boundaries. Because it is work, yes. To dominate the mind so that it does not dominate us. To change oneself so that everything changes. To quiet the mind so that it stops projecting limits and obstacles.

Unfortunately, there is no button to disconnect or reprogram the ego. We must walk the path back to our stillness and peace, working to transcend this programming. Peace of mind is the most valuable thing we could obtain in our life, because what good is anything if we are not at peace with it? But we cannot buy this peace, nor will we suddenly find it, nor can it be given to us from the outside. However, we are fortunate that the yogis devoted thousands of years to study how to do this work and left us some of that wisdom in writing. Now we have a method to reach that supreme good which is serenity. We can have it and apply it in our life or in our climbing.

The proposal: the 8 steps

Yoga is presented as a solution to stop mental chatter. A path of self-knowledge through which to get rid of beliefs and conditioning to free ourselves from suffering, which is, to a large extent, generated by our own mind. It is a tool to dismantle the mental constructs that have been developed and installed in your mind over the years but which, at the same time, shape the walls of the prison that limits you. These mental constructs are in turn the root of all mental chatter, they are the foundation on which they lie. For example, if we perceive a route as difficult or of a higher grade than we believe to be fit for, we will treat it as such and we will be nervous, agitated, find it difficult to concentrate and waste our energy. That mental construct —the grade of the route or that someone told you it was difficult; remember that conditioning almost always comes from the outside— acts as conditioning and, as such, it influences, it permeates the whole experience. However, if you face the same route without that conditioning, it is more likely that you will be able to climb it more fluidly and spontaneously, as well as being more objective with the difficulty of the pitches. I am not saying that by not knowing the grade you will succeed, but at least, if you don't focus on that, you won't be predisposed to fail. Most likely, if the route is hard, you will fall anyway, but the reason for your failure will be clearer and, therefore, you will be able to work on it better. This is just one example among many that could be cited and that I will be citing throughout this exploration of yoga through climbing. I understand climbing as a perfect tool to bring to light our deepest conditioning in order to be able to work on them until they are overcome. And so, they stop projecting limits on us that, although they are imaginary —mental constructs— they become —we make them be— very real in many aspects of our lives. Moreover, this yogic approach to climbing can also be used to climb better because there is no denying that a clearer mind, free of fluctuations and dispersions and able to concentrate is an immense help for any activity, and even more so for climbing, where the mental component is so important.

> "Do your work within the peace of yoga and, free from selfish desires, be not moved in either success or failure. Yoga is peacefulness of mind —a peace that is ever the same."
>
> 2.48 Bhagavad Gita[2]

Although yoga has several tools, techniques and methods to achieve this goal of mental purification, it is rarely presented as a simple and/or systematized path. What was meant to bring clarity ends up

---
[2] Translation by Juan Mascaró

bringing more confusion in many of the people who go in search of it. Yoga has evolved over thousands of years. Imagine what could have happened to an entire philosophy that has been transmitted (in many cases orally) through time (thousands of years) and space (thousands of kilometers) if we barely remember what happened last year. We could say that it has been interpreted, reinterpreted, adapted, distorted, contaminated and refined over thousands of years until now. Today we have a jumble of names and styles of yoga. It is quite difficult to elucidate the true essence of yoga amidst all this circus.

Although the way in which yoga has entered the West has been through a physical practice, through the postures —called *asanas*—, the work on the body is a small part of yoga, being in its essence mostly an inner, spiritual path. The same happens in climbing, where many people have entered for the physical aspect, to get a stronger body or because they have seen impressive photos on social networks. But, in the end, the part that makes someone stay, regardless of how tight the climbing shoes are or how much the toes or the fingers hurt, is the mental component, the self-improvement, the satisfaction and inner growth it provides. Although this part is more subtle, and this process takes place almost imperceptibly for the climbers themselves.

Every time we hear the word yoga the conditioning of our western mind makes us think of people doing postures. But the truth is that the physical practice is so small within the vast philosophy of yoga that many of the great yogis of history spent their lives without doing any postures. There are different "yoga types" or paths of yoga that have been practiced throughout history. The different subgroups, paths or currents tend to be grouped under the following types: *karma* yoga (yoga of action), *bhakti* yoga (yoga of devotion), *jnana* yoga (yoga of knowledge or wisdom), *raja* yoga (mental yoga or meditation) and *hatha* yoga (yoga of physical practice).

Each yogi, each teacher or each school has a different way of seeing and living yoga, almost always resulting in a combination of the different branches to a greater or lesser extent. Almost all yoga types known under different names that are practiced today in the West are variations of hatha yoga, mixed or spiced with aspects from other branches. It is even mixed with other disciplines that have nothing to do with the path of yoga and that, in some cases, respond more to marketing, fashion or the teacher's own desire to enhance their ego by creating their own style.

This does not mean that all modern or adulterated yoga types are bad or lack benefits. I believe that all those who respect the background of yoga in one way or another are part of the continuous process of interpretation and adaptation. Each person has their own path and can follow the path that they consider best at any given moment. In fact, that is what we are doing. We are walking the path of yoga through climbing, applying the wisdom of yoga to our climbing to understand and deepen both the yogic wisdoms and the climbing, as well as our own self-knowledge.

Returning to the history of yoga, —which, like all history, is also circular— what is happening now has already happened before. Because the schools and styles of yoga have already multiplied infinite times in the past. At some point in this process of multiplication and synthesis, a sage named Patanjali appeared. This sage took the different currents or paths of yoga mentioned above and made a compilation of the wisdoms and organized them all in the form of Sutras (short verses or aphorisms). This compilation gave rise to what is known as the eight limbs of yoga, collected in the book of the Yoga Sutras.[3]

> 2.29 The eight limbs of yoga are yama, niyama, asana, pranayama, pratyahara, dharana, dhyana and samadhi.
>
> *Yoga Sutras*, Patanjali

These limbs constitute an integral system in which

---

[3] The Yoga Sutras, being originally written in Sanskrit and being short guidelines as well as deep and ambiguous, admit a great variety of interpretations and meanings. The quotes from the Yoga Sutras that you will find throughout this book correspond to an interpretation of the author, based on the study of various sources, both from the original text and from translations and commentaries, adapting them to the context to which they refer in each part of the book in order to bring them closer to the reader, without deviating from the meanings agreed upon by the various interpretations. You will find some recommended texts for further reading at the end of this book.

each of the steps, although presented separately for better understanding, is one of the branches of the same tree. That is to say, the steps are part of the same system and, therefore, each one of them in turn influences and includes the others. It could be said that they should be simultaneous, not consecutive. However, the best way to start is to consciously implement them one by one. That is to say, they should be progressively studied and integrated.

From here, we will see how we can go through these eight limbs through climbing, adapting as much as possible these precepts to our "scenario", so that they are accessible and applicable to us and see if we can reach a deeper level both climbing walls and in understanding ourselves and yoga. Always with the ultimate goal of reaching our purest essence, freeing us from the turbulences of the mind.

Yamas

The *yamas* are the basic moral codes for walking the path of yoga. They are sometimes referred to as restrictions or limits. And they are, since much of our reality is created both by what we allow for ourselves and by what we restrict or limit ourselves to. Let's say that these precepts provide the ethical framework within which to develop any practice. It has always been said that climbing serves to break our limits, but here we must clarify that limits and limitations are not always a negative thing, although they are sometimes seen as such. They can be negative when we allow limitations to be dictated by our lower self, our ego, which will place them wherever it suits it so that everything stays within its reach. For example, being overcome by laziness is a limit set by the lower self. Instead of training or going to the mountain, we find ourselves trapped in front of the screen, in a comfort that slowly consumes us. On the other hand, a limit set on the basis of an ethic, of an underlying wisdom, is to recognize when one's muscles and mind are exhausted and one needs to rest, even if that means giving up one's plans. Resting when one needs it could correspond, for example, to the first yama, ahimsa, non-violence (toward oneself, in this example).

Ahimsa

As I said, *ahimsa* is the principle of nonviolence. Generally, most of us do not consider ourselves to be violent, but this is not always the case. The main obstacle to eliminating violence is not recognizing violence. When ego and society have set the benchmark for what is violent and what is not, the spectrum is so narrow and has become so normalized that it is likely that the only thing we consider violent is physical violence toward other people. But there are many more forms of violence that are far more subtle, but no less harmful. There can be violence in words, thoughts, actions or omissions. There can be violence on others, on ourselves —whether it is our body or our mind— or on the environment in which we find ourselves. If you are walking to the sector and you step off the path, you are exercising violence on the environment. If you do not respect the nesting of birds, even if it is out of ignorance, you are exercising violence. And, as violence begets violence, it is possible that these continuously repeated acts may bring with them a rather aggressive regulation in the sector where we climb, to give an example that is becoming almost a daily occurrence.

> 2.35 When you settle in nonviolence (*ahimsa*), hostility fades around you.
>
> *Yoga Sutras*, Patanjali

What lies inside of us will reflect outside. If we project violence, we receive violence. And, conversely, if we let go of violence, everything will become more peaceful and friendly around us. For example, if we speak badly to someone, they will respond badly to us and create agitation, but if we speak kindly to them, we will get friendly and helpful responses.

It is important to be aware of the violence in which we live. Violence always comes back to us. We can even say that it also comes back multiplied. Breaking the cycle and getting out of the game may not be easy, but it is urgent. Another example of violence in climbing can be any situation in which the ego pushes us to climb harder. This may be rooted in comparing ourselves to others or to high standards relative to the grade we would like to climb. This pressure can lead to more violence in the form of injuries. Injuries that are the result of not respecting our body. Or that take the form of various frustrations that arise from not respecting our process in general. These attitudes, far from making us progress faster, make us bounce back and have to start from the bottom again and again. In a culture where overexertion is so highly valued, forcing oneself is something normal and accepted. This does not mean that it is healthy or even productive. The yogi/climber must be attentive to see where they are exerting any kind of violence so they can redirect themselves toward a more balanced life that will bring better and more satisfying results. They will do this by choosing less violent paths that reach the same places, respecting themselves and others and making more conscious decisions. On this path, we do not base our lives on fear, competitiveness, ignorance, anger or any other negative emotion. In the end, these types of behaviors are always the source of any violence. So much so that you don't know where one begins and the other ends. For example, you don't know if someone is violent because they are ignorant or ignorant because they are violent. Or if they are violent because they are afraid or they are afraid because they are violent and are always waiting for that violence to come back at them. It is important to look for and eliminate our inclination to violence, no matter how small it may be or what we believe it to be, and one way to find it is to observe our reactions, our automatisms, those that can make us manifest violence of any kind.

It should be said that being non-violent does not mean that we cannot be firm or oppose certain things. It is part of respecting ourselves not to allow anyone to be violent toward us, just as it is part of respecting others and the environment not to allow anyone or anything to be violent toward them.

Although the above examples try to show where there may be some subtle violence in our activity, it seems to me that climbing, probably because it is so firmly linked to nature, is already generally inclined toward non-violence. Already its ethical codes promote the highest standards of respect for the environment. The climber tries to impact the environment as little as possible. Climbers have a tendency to support each other and to facilitate or stimulate each other's growth.

This first *yama* also serves as a seat for the others, develops within them, and permeates the ethical ideas and behaviors discussed in the following *yamas*.

Satya

Satya could be defined as truthfulness, honesty. To always seek, tell and defend the truth as part of our path. In the West we say that a lie has no legs, but the reality is that the one who has no legs is the liar. Lies always end up trapping them and their life ends up becoming a total lie, a self-deception. A good example of where *satya* can be applied in climbing is grades. What good would it do a climber to lie about the grade they climb? Only to inflate their ego in front of others, and perhaps to convince themselves. The only result will be that it will cost them more to actually reach that grade if they think they have already achieved it. Or worse, one day they may find themselves in trouble climbing a route of the grade they say they are in. Another case is when we actually manage to reach a grade, but we know in our hearts that it was too easy for that level. We can fool ourselves into believing that we are ready. Or we can be honest with ourselves and keep working.

This has been happening all the time in sport climbing lately when high-level routes are starting to be repeated: they are being upgraded or downgraded, which doesn't mean that the first grader was lying and the second grader is right. All this hints at how subjective grading is and why it is so important to always keep in mind the process of searching for the truth in everything we do.

It is a search inasmuch as truth is always buried under our conditioning and misperceptions, and it is a conscious effort to seek the most objective, most real truth. What is true for one person may not be true for another, although in the minds of both people it is an almost absolute and automatic matter. In this case, we should prioritize the first *yama* on non-violence and not impose our truth on any person or use the truth to hurt others. If someone is happy having managed to climb a path of a certain grade, who are you to poison their happiness by telling them that this path is too easy for that grade? Maybe it is too easy for you, but for that person it is a great achievement. *Satya*'s truth cannot be destructive, it must be constructive. Then, if they indeed discover that it was too easy, they will have to keep looking for a way to keep progressing and to get out of their self-deception. In any case, honesty invites to seek truth, not as something that can be achieved once and for all, but as a process in which one does not deceive oneself or others.

> 2.36 When one is grounded in truth, what one does and what results correspond to it.
>
> *Yoga Sutras*, Patanjali

Climbing has always relied heavily on this principle. *Satya* has always been part of the ethical code of climbers and mountaineers. No one except the climber themselves could confirm whether they had reached a peak or not. Few people can confirm whether someone has actually sent the route they claim to have sent. The system has generally been to rely on people's honesty. So, there is supposed to be a commitment to truth and honesty, to not appropriating what does not belong to us, as developed in the following *yama, asteya.*

Asteya

Asteya is one of the basic pillars of any society or religion. It is commonly interpreted as not stealing. In a broader sense it could be said that it consists of not taking what does not belong to you or what does not belong to you or to others. As for most people living in western societies where private property is so important, we tend to interpret this precept as not taking other people's material goods. However, in yoga and philosophy it takes on a broader meaning, applying also to non-material or intangible things. Thus, it extends over a wide range of situations. It can be stealing someone's time or wasting it; taking someone's love, affection or friendship without reciprocating; abusing trust, taking someone else's ideas or projects, not giving fair credit for something someone has done; taking too many privileges or hoarding resources, etc.

In climbing, this principle is always present, as it's been since the very beginning: how important is it to give credit to those who accompanied you to the top? How important is it to respect and maintain in good condition the fixed material of the route since, once it has been fixed to the rock, it belongs to the whole community? How important is it not to hoard resources such as routes or sectors so that other people can enjoy them or other species can proliferate? As you can see, it is something much broader than the simple "thou shalt not steal". Nor is it overly complicated to discern when we might be overstepping the boundaries of this principle. When we do not crave what does not belong to us or what is not for us, we can find what is within our reach. That is, when we stop grasping and chasing after things, we make room for them to come.

> 2.37 For the one who is not inclined to take what does not belong to him, what is most valuable comes to him.
>
> *Yoga Sutras*, Patanjali

If you chase a cat it will never let itself be caught. But if you are doing your thing, it will probably come to you. It's the same when we stop imitating someone else's moves on a route. We can discover the moves that really suit us according to our capabilities or style. That is, when your mind is calm and you stop chasing what doesn't belong to you, what does belong to you emerges.

APARIGRAHA

> 1.39 When ambition ceases, true purpose appears.
>
> *Yoga Sutras*, Patanjali

This *yama* is often interpreted as non-ambition or non-greed. It does not mean that we should repress this impulse toward growth. What we should do is to control the desires for possession, accumulation or hoarding. This *yama* is a continuation of the previous one because, while *asteya* is not taking what is not ours, in *aparigraha* it would refer to not even desiring it. Greed can make us cling too tightly to external things, making us focus on absurd goals imposed by the lower self (conditioned by society, the immediate environment, the media, etc.). Because of our greed, skillfully fed by marketing and the consumer society, we work and produce so we can keep consuming things we don't need and that don't even do us any good. Moreover, sometimes we are even diverted away from the things that are beneficial to us. We may think, for example, that we will climb better when we have spent more money on stuff, focusing on the shell, instead of looking for what limits us within ourselves.

Another example of ambition traps in climbing can be seen in "grade collectors". In their ambition to aim for more and more routes they stop enjoying climbing, they lose the sense of what they are doing. It is not necessary for everyone to interpret climbing as self-knowledge and self-realization, but the ego should not cloud our minds with its desire to be the strongest, the one who has done the most grades or the one who has climbed the most routes or mountains. I don't think that's what it's all about, although it sometimes seems so. Generally, and even more so in this age of social networks, we tend to compare ourselves with others and covet other people's things almost without realizing it. We want to climb where others climb, travel where others travel or train on the climbing walls where others train. This way of coveting other people's things makes us lose sight of what we have, of what we are. In other words, it takes us away from ourselves and our purpose. We divide our energies, we pursue absurd things without even being aware that we are pursuing them.

Brahmacharya

This is one of the most controversial concepts, mainly because it is one of the most uncomfortable for the ego. It is usually interpreted as moderation or sexual abstinence or, rather, keeping the mind free of erotic ideas. This, which a priori sounds too monastic, has some interpretations more accessible to anyone. I do not believe that it is necessary to renounce sex to maintain vital energies or to be able to self-realize, but what is advisable is to stop being a slave of sexual impulses. This is much more reasonable. The purpose of yoga is to free us from everything that enslaves us, and sex is something that can enslave us if the energies are not properly controlled. As we have already seen in the previous paragraphs, one should not allow oneself to be conditioned by the objects and ambitions of the self, nor by the lower sexual impulses.

> 1.38 With moderation comes vitality.
>
> *Yoga Sutras*, Patanjali

We all know the typical person who is only moved by sexual interest. We see them always circling around people they consider potential sexual partners. I wouldn't want to force this into climbing, but we've all seen people who only go out of their way to help or share their climbing with people they find attractive or who arouse some kind of sexual interest in them. Making climbing revolve around sexual urges is a lousy use of the potential this activity has. That is why in this *yama,* as in the previous ones, it is a matter of setting appropriate limits. To be alert so that, without repressing oneself, we do not get carried away by passions to the point of clouding our mind, objectifying others or losing our way and our priorities. Understood more subtly, it can be said that moderation and self-control could be characteristics derived from the exercise of both this *yama* and the previous one (*aparigraha*, non-covetousness). When energies are well-oriented and concentrated they multiply, gaining more vitality and vigor. That is, we may be able to moderate our energies (of any kind) and direct them inward. To the search for peace of mind and happiness, and not to the wastefulness of being continually focused on the external, trying to satisfy desires and ambitions or seeking external validation or recognition. It can be said that in this control of energies one has to choose what to feed with these energies: whether the lower ego that seeks status and social recognition or the higher self that is in search of peace and happiness.

Niyamas

If the *yamas* are precepts and limits not to generate more impurities, the *niyamas* come to show the way to the most basic of the purification and refinement of the being. Both, *yama* and *niyama*, are the solid foundation on which lays the rest of the path. Rather, the shoes we will use to walk it —the approach shoes, as we could call them in our context.

Saucha

All purification requires cleansing, and in this case and as in everything that surrounds yoga, it does not only refer to the body or objects. It also refers to the mind and emotions. *Saucha* comes to be translated as cleansing. Cleansing in a very broad sense, as a concept that applies to everything, starting with the most obvious, that of cleansing the body. And since we have started with the external, it should be said that it also applies to the environment. There is no need to talk about the importance of keeping the environment clean or having equipment in good condition, for our safety and that of others, for example.

Where this precept becomes more interesting is in the purity and cleanliness of the mind and emotions. This is where it is most difficult for us to carry out, perhaps because it is so subtle. It is much easier to dust off a table than to get rid of the smallest envy that can arise in our minds. However, it is something very necessary and urgent, since the mind impregnates the whole vital experience and if we don't "clean" it correctly it will end up staining everything. The impurities of the mind are, for example, negative thoughts, which create a negative attitude and therefore negative results. It is normal for negative thoughts to appear just as it is normal for dust to enter a house. So, the point is to do the conscious work of cleaning it when necessary (the mind and the house) and to be attentive. Because it is necessary to detect the sources of impurities and dirt in order to keep it clean for as long as possible.

> 2.41 With purification one gains mental clarity, focus and mastery of the senses, which predisposes one to happiness and self-realization.
>
> *Yoga Sutras*, Patanjali

A clear mind is necessary both to climb a route and to achieve fulfillment in any area of life. Just as you don't pee on the foot of the route, you also don't clutter your mind with unnecessary negative thoughts that can sabotage or cloud your experience. If you are afraid, doubtful, or anxious to outdo your partner, it is best not to climb the wall. Do your best to overcome them by relaxing your mind and purifying it. Focus on more positive emotions such as enjoying the experience as it is. In this way, you will also be able to apply the next *niyama* —*santosha*, contentment.

SANTOSHA

Santosha is translated as contentment. It is an attitude in which we remain in joy above the fluctuations of the mind which, like the fluctuations that they are, come and go, rise and fall. This contentment, this predisposition to joy and happiness does not come out of nowhere, it is a determination. It is a firm and conscious decision not to be dragged down by the negative, focusing on and inhabiting positive states of mind. It is the way we gain independence from external situations. It is the acceptance of what is there so that we do not cling to what is not there. We do not measure ourselves according to unrealistic expectations or hypothetical situations but live the present as it is. If you fall trying a route, you can let yourself be flooded with negativity and feelings of inferiority and condemn the rest of the session to failure. But you can also accept the situation as it is without identifying with it. That is, you are not a better or worse climber or stronger or weaker because you failed.

We experience contentment every time we go climbing and realize how simple life is, the enjoyment, the joy. Spending the day with friends, in nature, experimenting with ourselves, with our experiences, our sensations... However, we spend most of our time at the mercy of our absurd daily complications. We keep ourselves unhappy by continually pursuing things, letting our mind generate the suffering of not achieving them. If we do not train our mind in contentment it will continue to desire absurd things that we'll keep chasing after.

Could we extend this feeling of fullness, joy and contentment that we have in the simplicity of climbing to any moment of our life? Why not? This contentment is a determination, not an emotion. We have all seen people who suffer climbing as much as you suffer doing other things.

Wish you were somewhere else or complain you don't like the type of rock. Consider that the temperature is not optimal or you miss your couch and you will remain in suffering. Say goodbye to contentment and the perfection of the moment. Choose to accept and you will live in acceptance and contentment. Choose to reject and you will live in rejection and denial. This determination is made by putting the focus on the positive. Even if you fail a route or if the weather changes you can find something positive in the experience. You reach into a crack that you thought had a good grip and it turns out that it doesn't, that it's a larger sloper than it looked. Your mind, which is not very quick to be content and accept reality, starts looking for other grips or other positions instead of making good use of what it found, resulting in a much greater expenditure of energy leading to exhaustion. More mental agitation that ultimately leads to not being able to make the step.

Don't let your ego sabotage your time with its preconceived ideas and expectations that were left out of the reality of the moment. Contentment is on the inside, not on the outside, even if we sometimes link it to external situations that by nature are changeable and do not always fit our mental projections.

> 2.42 Through contentment arises supreme happiness
>
> *Yoga Sutras*, Patanjali

Like the others, this *niyama* is based on the previous precepts. Contentment appears only in a mind that is pure, non-covetous, free from desire, non-violent, honest and does not let its energies disperse. It is a mind that stands firm in its inner center. It does not allow itself to be swayed by external conditions, trusting and maintaining its clarity to make the best of what it finds and knowing that after a hard sequence a rest will come.

Tapas

Tapas is one of the most interesting and perhaps one of the most popular and controversial concepts. In some translations it is interpreted as austerity. But, while austerity may be a part of *tapas*, it is not all of it. It is a much broader concept. *Tapas* has also been interpreted as "heat", "warm" or "burn", which makes it even more confusing. The interpretation that is most convincing to me is "purification by fire". You burn all those mental projections that hinder you, you burn the limits and conditioning —going beyond them. Although it can also be interpreted as firmness or discipline, this also falls a little short. Discipline toward what? It is to persist in your efforts, without reaching exhaustion or overexertion, but without being self-indulgent. Without letting the ego put a ceiling over us, becoming our cage. It is the self-discipline we need to do what is hard. It is necessary for adversity to stop oppressing you, obstructing and limiting your growth.

Austerity is sometimes confused with the rejection of all comfort. *Tapas* is more about detachment from things. We don't let our attachments limit us. We do the work that needs to be done in order to grow. It is what is so popularly known today as "getting out of the comfort zone". Challenging ourselves, moving toward the limit so we can break free from it. To voluntarily exercise discomfort. That is why this concept cannot simply be limited to what we know as austerity. The practice of *tapas* is different according to the person and the path they're in. For one person it may be saying what they have to say and for another person it may be keeping quiet when they should remain silent. For another it may be eating less and for another it may be eating more or healthier. For one person it may be daring to do what they never dared to do while for another it may be to stop doing so many things. We have to keep on the lookout for ourselves to always find ways to grow by purifying what limits us.

> 2.43 When discipline (*tapas*) burns away impurities, the body and the senses are perfected.
>
> *Yoga Sutras*, Patanjali

Climbing is the perfect setting in which to practice *tapas*. It makes you aware of both your limits and the only way to overcome them: to move toward them. You start by being afraid of heights despite the safety of the equipment. This fear is transcended when you hang on the wall and see for yourself the safety and the sensation of being several meters high. The only way to overcome the fear of falling is to actually fall a few times, either as training or experiencing it directly. If you have a hard time slab climbing or overhang climbing or whatever it is that limits you, to overcome that limit, to burn it, you must go toward it. Expose yourself to its fire and let it burn away the parts of your mind that hinder you when you try to tackle a section you were "uncomfortable" with.

Tapas is the way to grow by overcoming all the obstacles that overshadow you, the ones that keep you in the confines of the comfort of the cage your ego has created for you. It is an attitude that moves you to overcome all that, to direct you to life and growth, without staying in the comfortable or remain within the barriers imposed by the ego (remember that the ego is not you, although we tend to identification, so these barriers have been imposed on you from the outside, but it is your job to remove them).

SVADHYAYA

This is the concept on which this whole series of books "Wisdom from the Rock" is based on. Applying wisdoms and philosophies to know oneself more deeply through climbing. This *niyama* refers to the study and knowledge of oneself. *Sva* means "self" and *adhyaya* means something like "lesson". Therefore, *Svadhyaya* could be "lesson of oneself". It is the self-study, self-observation, self-knowledge, self-analysis. It can be done in many ways such as reading, conversing, climbing, doing postures, observing reactions, investigating or, in short, deepening in everything that concerns oneself and one's path of realization. It can be, as you are doing now, studying wisdoms and philosophies that bring light to your life, that eliminate the shadows of the ego. If you have come this far, overcoming all the rejections that your ego may have toward something that threatens it, we can say that you are applying some *svadhyaya*.

> 2.44 Study yourself, discover your personal divinity.
>
> *Yoga Sutras*, Patanjali

The wisdoms, such as this one of yoga that we are studying, provide us with a map —which is not always very clear— to reach the deepest and purest part of ourselves. To the divine essence that is in each one of us, to our true potential. Because each of the things you will read in this book, or in the *Yoga Sutras* or in any yoga book, tend to the same end: to go filing the superficial layers and impurities to get to the essence, to your true self, which is infinite. Infinite as your possibilities. Thanks to the study of these texts, we will be able to find a foothold on ledges of wisdom that are a safe and stable place to continue our work, without being shaken by the daily nonsense in which we end up immersed most of the time.

It is not necessary to be a goody-goody and follow all the precepts to the letter, but it is good to give them a chance and try to integrate them into our lives. To delve into them as much as possible and to make them permeate through our life and our actions. To gain awareness of the purest truths without being carried away by the illusions and projections of the ego. When you get on the rock and observe your sensations, putting into practice whatever piece of wisdom you have been studying. When you observe the results and continue to experiment. When something doesn't go the way you wanted it to and instead of getting frustrated you observe yourself, your reactions or the causes of your reactions. You don't let yourself be dragged down by them. You use every situation to go deeper into yourself. After all, you are the one you are going to spend the rest of this life with.

ISHVARAPRANIDHANA

Ishvarapranidhana is popularly translated as surrender to God. It should be said that we are not necessarily talking about any particular god but rather about "something" higher than ourselves. Everyone can think here of their deity, spiritual goal or higher motivation. You can use any other term that helps you understand this *niyama* of "surrender" or "devotion". One can choose what to "surrender" to, be it destiny, the universe, a higher purpose or even an activity. What is important is to understand the question of surrendering one's action to something higher, setting aside selfish desires, the illusion of control and unrealistic expectations. What is important is the surrender itself, not to whom or what to surrender. Pure and selfless action, when we do not expect anything in return or are not attached to a result. It is all part of the path and all is equally important. We do what we must do and when we must do it, eliminating through this "surrender" the suffering of not achieving the expected results.

This allows us to do things without anxiety about the results, without expectations, leaving aside the calculating mind that divides between profit or loss, success or failure, sending or falling. We thus allow ourselves to perform each activity as if it were a game, or rather a celebration in itself. Afterwards, whatever must come, will come.

> 2.45 Through surrender, total integration is achieved.
>
> *Yoga Sutras*, Patanjali

When we climb a route we can surrender to it, to its lessons, to the experience, and commit to our personal development as climbers as we traverse it. However, if we put too much focus on sending the route (the result) we will probably be tense. We will make more forced moves and suffer frustration or disappointment if we don't get it or if it doesn't go the way we wanted. When we do things with an end in mind or expecting some kind of reward, the whole experience ends up being contaminated. Conditioned to those pre-established parameters that leave out a great part of what the experience in general can bring us. If you surrender yourself entirely to what you are doing, you will be able to keep your mind calm. You will be able to perform the action in a fluid way, according to what the moment asks for, accepting what comes without attachments or longings. In this way, you will know that everything is part of a path that is longer and bigger than you. You don't have to worry so much about the little obstacles you will encounter along the way (or on the route). At some point, as an indirect result of your actions, all your efforts will align toward the right sequences and movements. You will send the route. An interesting example can also be found in the popular saying "God willing". You are stuck on a step where you don't know if you will be able to make it to the next hold. However, instead of exhausting yourself by hanging on to the grip you have and feeding your doubts, you decide to throw your hand out and think "God willing". You surrender to what you are doing, detaching yourself from the outcome. If you make it, fine. If you fall, fine, you'll just try again.

Recap

This is all for the *yamas* and *niyamas*. As you can see, they are something like the "ten commandments". The most basic and universal concepts to build a good practice (of yoga or anything else) or even a good life in general (since our life is our practice). They are the gates through which one must enter yoga, the foundations that ground any other practice within the system. And to make it a little clearer, I want to make a synthesis that I hope can help you integrate them better. A brief "practical recap" through the example of climbers who have these codes present in some way in their climbing.

These climbers go out to their favorite climbing sector with the intention of exercising their mind and body on the rock, to practice their ability to remain mentally calm in all situations.

For this purpose, they have chosen a project that is slightly uncomfortable, somewhat beyond their capabilities, but which they believe will serve to discipline themselves and grow (*tapas*, self-discipline/challenging the ego). They will seek to send the route as the culmination of the path but will surrender to each of the experiences that the process brings them (*ishvarapranidhana*, surrender of action). In this way they will find joy in what the present brings them, without forming great expectations and focusing on the fullness of the experience (*santosha*, contentment). They will take good note of every lesson the rock can give them about themselves, their nature, their fears, their conditioning, their projections, etc. (*svadhyaya*, self-study). And, although situations will arise that may hurt their ego and provoke emotional reactions, they will try to keep their mind always clean of negative emotions that may taint their experience (*saucha*, cleanliness/purity).

After all, they are there stroking rocks to do their inner work. They cannot allow themselves to disperse their energies by letting any outside influence sidetrack them. However strong the distractions or temptations to impress others may be, it is not always the time to fall for it (*brahmacharya*, self-control/moderation). They must keep the focus on themselves, within themselves, without comparing themselves to others or coveting the journey of others. What difference does it make whether you are doing your work on a path of higher or lower grade than someone else (*aparigraha*, not coveting). Each one must accept what is given to them at any given moment, what is available to them. They must not spread themselves thin by trying to monopolize other people's projects or deny the space that others need to do their work. Belay another person when it is their turn, respect the right to use a common space among peers and with all the other species (*asteya*, do not accumulate/hoard).

Because the rock is such a great and wonderful thing that anyone should have access to do their "work" on it. Therefore, it is also part of our job to support every person who intends to grow by providing truthful and correct, useful and objective information. For example, inform about the grades, without misleading others and ourselves (to inflate our ego) about the difficulty of the routes (*satya*, truthfulness/honesty). Everything must be based on mutual respect, respect for the natural environment and respect for oneself and the harmonious development of inner growth, without forcing anything or anyone, least of all ourselves (*ahimsa*, non-violence).

Asana

Asana means posture, as you probably already know. This is the most popular part of yoga in the West. But, again, it is only a part of the system, a fragment. To get an idea of scale, we can say that of Patanjali's one hundred and ninety-six yoga sutras, only three refer to *asanas*. However, the sutras cannot be judged by their length or quantity. As you will see below, these three sutras are quite interesting, and we can find a curious parallel with climbing.

What yoga *asanas* and climbing have in common is that they are both a set of awkward postures. Through control of the body and mastery of the mind we must make them comfortable and stable. It is as simple as that. Both (climbing and yoga postures) are the means through which we experiment with our body and our sensations, gaining awareness of our own body and mastery over our own mind.

One of the main objectives is to strengthen peace of mind. For this, we put it to work in the strangest postures, whether on the horizontal mat or on the vertical rock. We exercise in the process of making the uncomfortable comfortable, as well as remaining stable in instability, thus expanding our ability to be comfortable in different positions (or situations).

> 2.46 The posture shall be firm and comfortable.
>
> *Yoga Sutras*, Paranjali

Here the ability to harmonize the opposites comes into play as the posture must be the perfect balance between tension and relaxation, between firmness and softness. The same applies to climbing. If, on the one hand, we are too tense and rigid, we will make awkward movements that will consume too much energy. In this way, there will be a greater risk of injury. If, on the other hand, we are too relaxed, it will be difficult to maintain our position on the wall and gravity will do the rest. This is the balance that is needed both for yoga postures and for life. Relaxed concentration, flexible firmness, tightening by releasing.

The yoga *asana* sequences that are usually practiced are composed of two moments. The *asana*, which is the stable posture (meaning something like "seat") and the *vinyasa*, which are the transitions between postures (chaining of postures).

Climbing a route is like a yoga sequence. You move up the wall into the posture (*vinyasa*) and then settle into it (*asana*). All the techniques you have learned and all the physical conditioning you have done serve you to maintain a firm and stable posture while you are on the wall, while visualizing the next step, while maintaining concentration or while resting. Then you move again (*vinyasa*) to the next position/rest/posture (*asana*). In climbing, this process of action (*vinyasa*) and stable posture (*asana*) can be done in very short time intervals —even in milliseconds—, while in yoga they are usually slower and mostly sustained movements.

Although in climbing the postures are held for less time —although sometimes these "rests" or "*asanas*" can also last several minutes— the objective is the same: the personal experimentation of one's own body, its possibilities and its limitations. We deepen concentration and self-knowledge while working on keeping the mind calm even in the most uncomfortable postures and situations.

Thus, both climbing and yoga postures are a tool for both personal development and self-awareness. Personal development because it is based on one's own experience. When climbing we experiment with different techniques, different positions, different movements and, in short, with different ways of using the body. All this forces us to transcend mental limits and discomfort. Self-awareness because it is necessary to develop a greater awareness of what we are doing. It is necessary to abandon the automatisms that govern our life without realizing it. For example, without letting the ego dictate to us how a movement is done or making us do it wrong impulsively without considering the demands of the situation at hand.

> 2.47 The *asana* is perfected when all effort is relaxed and the attention is integrated in the infinite.
>
> *Yoga Sutras*, Paranjali

When we get hold of a technique, a grip or a foothold and the posture becomes bearable, we begin to have the capacity to even rest in it when previously we could hardly rest from there. And so, with practice, we manage to make resting on the rock comfortable and stable. Rest that allows us to relax and helps us to better manage the energy we will need to complete the route. In the same way that the practice of *asanas* allows us to deepen in a position of the body until it becomes firm and our mind remains relaxed in it. For a body and mind that remain always in comfort, the slightest discomfort can have catastrophic consequences —such as physical and/or mental illness. A mind and body trained in yoga or climbing develops its peace of mind and physical strength in such a way that it can transcend discomfort, stress, fear, or fatigue, just to name a few. For example, when you climb a route of a grade that you have consolidated, you will be able to observe how these pairs of opposites —comfortable/uncomfortable, easy/difficult, good or bad holds, etc.— have already ceased to be part of the experience. This means that you have transcended them at those levels, although it will not be difficult for you to remember how hard it was to transcend them when you were working to reach that level.

> 2.48 Then, the pairs of opposites cease to disturb.
>
> Yoga Sutras, Paranjali

Yoga postures are not the design of the gods. Even more remarkable is that they have been developed and perfected over the centuries by yogis who, through observation and experimentation with their own bodies, have designed a multitude of *asanas* and combinations that can be loaded with meaning. They have specific objectives for the healing of the body, to promote specific physiological processes or even imply some mythological meaning. By this, I mean that it is not my intention to downgrade the importance or benefits of yoga *asanas*, I simply wanted to make whoever is reading this see the parallelism between both "activities". The main difference, and that which brings their nuances, is the medium (vertical or horizontal). Therefore, although I believe they are essentially the same thing, they can also complement each other well. They give to the practice, through which we strengthen the body and our mind, a wide and balanced range of tools and instruments in the form of postures and transitions.

If you are interested in going deeper into this complementarity, there are several very interesting books on climbing and *asana*. As I understand it, the way to make the physical part of climbing more yogic is simply to pay more attention to our body and put more intention in what we do on the wall. Deepening the improvement of the stability and comfort of the posture —whatever it is, even if we are resting on a small crimp doing opposition with your legs or any other movement you can think of—. Reconciling the opposites in a harmonic way and making the transitions in the most precise and conscious way possible, optimally coordinating the parts of our body while keeping our mind focused and serene.

Pranayama

Pranayama is the next step after *asana*. In this step we focus on controlling our breath and our energy. *Prana* means breath, but also energy. Interestingly, this term encompasses both. Throughout this chapter we will reflect on why. *Ayama* means control, mastery, regulation, but also extension or expansion. Therefore, *Pranayama* can be interpreted as both breath regulation and energy regulation, while it can also be energy (or breath) expansion.

In climbing, it is easy to observe how our breathing fluctuates. When we are agitated or in tension (physical or mental) our breath becomes agitated, choppy and shallow. A good example is the famous huffing and puffing that indicates when someone is "giving it their all" on the wall.

Conversely, when our mind is calm and our body is in good position, we breathe calmly and deeply. But which came first, the breathing or the mental calm? This is what yogis have experienced through *pranayama*: that it is a bidirectional and reversible process. That is, if you have a calm mind, your breath will be calm. Likewise, if you calm your breath, you can calm your mind. Breathing is the bridge between the body and the mind. The formula would be as follows: by learning to regulate the breath we will be able to quiet and calm the mind as well as be able to regulate or extend our energies. And by extending or expanding our energy we can understand to make a more efficient use of them, a more optimal management. Although controlling the breath is not at all easy and its control requires intention and discipline, it is easier than controlling the mind, which when agitated there is no way to get a grip on it. Breathing is a good starting point, something tangible and measurable from which to begin to control the mind. The point from which to start untangling the rope. For example, if we are climbing and we come to a rest, but we keep our breathing agitated (and our mind agitated) after making a hard step, perhaps, even if we are in a comfortable and resting position, we will not manage to recover the energy and stillness of the mind without first relaxing our breathing. Therefore, we will continue climbing the next sequences of the route with lower energy levels. On the contrary, if we take a moment to strengthen our posture at rest and concentrate on breathing deeply and calmly, we will be able to recover our energy faster, as well as calm our mind and free it from the tension accumulated in the previous steps. This will allow us to start the next section of the route with freshness, thus expanding the possibilities of our energies.

> 2.49 When the steady and stable posture (*asana*) is achieved, the breath (*pranayama*) can be controlled.
>
> *Yoga Sutras*, Paranjali

It is understood that the steps of yoga are consecutive and that the next one always encompasses the previous one. But in this case Patanjali specifies it explicitly in the first sutra that talks about *pranayama*. We have said that *asana* is the stable and comfortable posture (regardless of how uncomfortable it may seem or if we are hanging on a wall). Therefore, it is understood that to start practicing *pranayama* we must start from that stability and comfort. And it is difficult to do otherwise. Imagine that you have started to control your breathing just right when you are pushing through on a complicated step or at the edge of your strength at the end of the route. It's already hard to stay at least half-concentrated on what you're doing. However, as soon as you have a chance to do an *asana*-rest, to find a stable posture within the instability, you can make it stable and comfortable enough to rest and concentrate on managing your breath, so that you can relax and rest more, expanding your energy "budget" for the rest of the route.

> 2.50 *Pranayama* is composed of inhalation, exhalation and retention. It becomes spacious and gentle by regulating the time, number and object of focus.
>
> *Yoga Sutras*, Paranjali

This is not a how-to book, so we will not delve into the hundreds of techniques that exist according to different purposes or personal choices. The techniques consist of the combination of inhalation, exhalation and retention. They take into account the duration of these, whether they are performed more deeply or more superficially, more from the chest or more from the abdomen, among many other variables. There are different types of *pranayama,* both to activate the energies and to relax (or calm the mind). It is interesting to investigate and experiment with them until we find the one that works best for us. Personally, to relax the tension of the mind when I rest on the route, I usually experiment with simple and effective breaths, such as inhale, hold, exhale and hold in intervals of four seconds each. Repeating this process several times stabilizes the breath and, therefore, the posture and the mind. Even if you had to climb with great effort in the previous steps, you will be able to begin the following sequence with a serene mind, freed from the tensions (fears, insecurities) generated in the previous steps. Or the most basic one, which would be simply to inhale five seconds and exhale ten. The time estimation is secondary. The important thing is that the exhalation is twice as long as the inhalation. Another interesting breath technique may be "breath of fire" (consisting of a rapid inhalation and exhalation, followed by a retention of several seconds), which serves to stimulate the energies. It could be done while at rest, moments before facing the most difficult part of the route. This would be somewhat more advanced and requires previous mastery of the basics.

To practice *pranayama* in climbing, I would recommend starting to practice on a route that, although demanding, you already know or have somehow mastered. We will use it to experiment with the different techniques, putting them into practice, experiencing them in body and mind. In this way, we can observe the powerful effects that the regulation of breathing has, and we can gradually discover new tools, as yogis have always done. By proceeding in this way, we will be able to find the techniques and combinations that work best for us. The goal is to keep practicing until we integrate them effortlessly into our climbing (and life) without having to pay attention to how much we inhale, exhale or hold, as the following sutra indicates:

> 2.51 A fourth type of *pranayama* transcends internal and external conditions.
>
> *Yoga Sutras*, Paranjali

At this point we will have succeeded in re-educating our breathing and we will be able to use the most appropriate one at each moment, unconsciously, regulating it without effort and keeping ourselves in optimal conditions independently of the internal or external conditions. Usually, if we have not practiced or brought our intention to this before, we tend, also unconsciously, to let the breath (and therefore the mind) work in an automatic, wild and chaotic way. The result is an agitation that is not good for a time when relaxation should predominate. This causes a lack of control and a disharmony that harms our climbing and our life, making us victims of our agitation and dispersion of energies instead of being the masters of our own breathing, capable of efficiently using our energies and directing our mind.

2.52 *Pranayama* removes the veil that covers the inner light.

Yoga Sutras, Paranjali

Thanks to the handling of *pranayama*, the foundations are laid to get rid of the mental dispersions that cloud our perception and "veil" reality. It is the step through which, using this body-mind bridge, we can quieten and empty the mind of its fluctuations and projections that do not let us see reality as it is —such as fears of falling or failing or the desire to send the route; the desire for recognition or the typical aversions of climbing such as, "I don't like this rock" or "the footholds are bad"—, among others. If we calm our mind and free it from these projections, we will be able to better visualize the route and climb it more accurately than if our perception is clouded and conditioned with fears, expectations, preferences, etc. This stillness and stopping of mental chatter through *pranayama* is a prerequisite for progress, both in a climbing route and in the route of yoga and opens the door to the next steps of the yoga method.

> 2.53 And the mind becomes able to concentrate.
>
> *Yoga Sutras*, Paranjali

Pratyahara

Pratyahara is known as the control of the senses. This is the last step regarding the external aspects of yoga. It is the starting point (after observing the previous steps) for the retreat toward our inner self. It is the last step of the most practical part of the Yoga Sutras (the *sadhana pada*), from which more internal experiences are dealt with, as we will see in the following steps of yoga (*vibhuti pada*).

The five senses are the gateways from the outer to the inner world, so if we want to master our mind, we should not let it be affected by every external thing. External impressions and stimuli are food for our mind, so we must choose what we want to feed on to achieve our purposes. Just as we eat healthy foods to improve our fitness and avoid fatty or processed foods, we must consciously configure our "diet" of impressions.

By working the previous step (*pranayama*) we could get our mind calm. But we will have a hard time keeping it that way if we are not able to retract our senses and prevent them from chasing the abundant amount of external stimuli that are constantly around us.

Mastering the senses consists not so much in repressing them as in orienting them toward our purpose. That is to say, we do not let them wildly run around engaging with any stimulus that comes our way, but rather we determine what we want to perceive and what we do not want to perceive.

> 2.54 *Pratyahara* is when the senses become detached from external conditions and become aligned with the mind and its purpose.
>
> *Yoga Sutras*, Paranjali

We could describe *pratyahara* as taming our senses to let in only the information that is useful to us and that is aligned with our purposes and not with the attachments of the ego. If we do not control our senses, the ego will. Let's see how this can be easily tested in climbing. If you control your senses and align them with your purpose for climbing a route, they will help you see the best way to approach a pitch. We will be able to identify the best holds, feel the rock for useful subtle cracks to reinforce our grip or for friction points that allow our feet to grip the rock, etc. However, if we do not control our senses, they will run free following any stimulus or, even worse, reinforcing our ego's fears. Thus, someone talking at the foot of the route can become a distraction, the weather being a little hot or cold can be a good excuse for not advancing, or how tightly my climbing shoes are squeezing my toes can become the protagonist of the climbing experience. We must tame the senses so that they work for us, not against us. We need to be able to withdraw our awareness from negative and unnecessary stimuli, reinforcing the positive ones that we can use to achieve our purpose.

> 2.55 The result of *Pratyahara* is the mastery over the senses.
>
> *Yoga Sutras*, Paranjali

We can direct our senses wherever we want and make them be at our service. With this discipline we stop being slaves to them (I'm cold, it smells bad —or it smells good and I'm hungry—, it's tight, it's too noisy, I'm going to check Instagram, and so on and so forth). We can choose where to focus. The goal is for them to serve our growth, not our stagnation. If we indulge in full sense gratification, we will be continually serving our more short-termist impulses, besides the fact that it will never end. This is precisely what stagnation is. Permanence in the same situations, at the same levels. We won't advance if, while climbing, we are continually looking only for the "good" holds, filling our hands with chalk or listening to or even participating in conversations with the people at the foot of the route or around us. Think of it this way, even reading an interesting book would take us too long and we would understand little if we constantly fell into the impulse to check social media.

Mastery of the senses leads us to be able to become independent of external conditions, which makes us gain freedom —and thus move toward liberation, toward independence from conditioning—. It is not easy, but it is worth being alert to when we are allowing ourselves to be dragged by the senses and taking the opportunity to put our mastery into practice.

Dharana

This is the step laying the groundwork for the last three steps, the inner steps. In turn, these final steps are something like a consequence or result of what has been practiced in the first five steps. In other words, the first five steps prepare you for the inner path that unfolds in the last three: *dharana*, *dhyana* and *samadhi*.

Dharana is concentration. Thus, it is the preliminary step to meditation (*dhyana*).

> 3.1 Concentration (*dharana*) is the fixation of the mind on one point (or object, idea or activity).
>
> *Yoga Sutras*, Paranjali

The mind is accustomed to wildly jump from one object or idea to another, uncontrollably and in a matter of seconds. The ability of an untrained mind to focus is more than limited.

I'm sure you've already experimented with different degrees of concentration in your climbing. There are days when you are able to concentrate on what you are doing and your climbing seems to have significantly improved. You are able to move with precision and maintain the calmness that allows you to flow up the wall. Then there are days when you are scattered and your movements on the wall become clumsy and imprecise. In fact, Patanjali already pointed out in the early sutras what the effects of a scattered mind were:

> 1.31 As a result of mental distraction, pain, desperation, body trembling and agitated breathing appear.
>
> *Yoga Sutras*, Paranjali

It's funny, because here he mentions something we climbers have all experienced at one point or another: body trembling. In fact, we have our own jargon to define it: the "Elvis leg" or the "sewing machine leg." These are a couple of ways of defining this tremor that comes over our leg due to a distracted or overly tense mind (agitated or unfocused by fear, for example). In previous chapters, we have also talked about agitated breathing (the famous huffing and puffing we used as an example), which can be, in turn, a symptom of distraction, of lack of full concentration.

Well, climbing is not only useful as an example or to measure whether we are dispersed or concentrated. It also serves as mental training to exercise this ability to concentrate. You can choose what you want to concentrate on and make sure that your concentration remains in line with what you have set out to do. For example, to send a route, you can focus your concentration on the sequences you have to develop. On the parts of your body involved, on your breathing, on the sensations that each hold gives you, or simply on keeping your mind clear. Your mind will always try to sabotage you if you don't keep it focused on what you want it to. If you don't dominate it, it will dominate you. Remember that climbing, as yoga, is a yoke for the mind, a tool to subdue the mind. And your mind knows it and does not want to be subdued. As soon as you start climbing, if you don't sharpen your concentration, the egoic mind will start to get in the way, throwing out all sorts of excuses at you to convince you to get off the wall, such as fears that prevent you from making the moves you have planned or distractions caused by any aspect that can pull you out of your endeavor. It could be thoughts such as the bolts are too far apart, these grips are too bad, I'm not at this grade yet, yesterday I had a sore finger so it'll get on the way today, etc. That's the work of the mind/ego; to keep you in comfort and stagnation at any cost. Anything that sounds like growth/discomfort/unknown will be furiously sabotaged with every weapon available. But there you will be, working to bring it back to your purpose, in this case climbing the route. And no matter how many times it has to be brought back, the important thing is to be alert and do it when it needs to be done. The mind has to be tamed, it's like a dog. The untamed dog will ignore all commands and go after whatever comes its way (other dogs, any person or any smell), whether or not it is aligned with the purpose. However, with time and the right education, the dog will begin to obey commands and will not chase what it is not supposed to chase. The dog will even be able to sit and stay sitting in one place when their owner tells him to. The ability to maintain focus and concentration is essential to be your own master, the master of your life, being able to stay seated on what you want without being carried away by the impulses of your mind/ego. When you achieve this state and can maintain concentration for longer periods of time, you will enter the next step, meditation.

Dhyana

3.2 When concentration is maintained uninterrupted it is meditation (*dhyana*).

Yoga Sutras, Paranjali

In the previous step (*dharana*) one strives to concentrate on something concrete. It eliminates distractions and fluctuations when they appear to keep the mind focused. In this step the concentration is already settled. It is maintained in a more constant and deeper way and at the same time it can permeate everything that is being done (not just a part of it, as we talked in the previous chapter about concentrating on the breath or on the movements). Thus, this kind of expanded concentration becomes meditation. It is that simple —although not easy. It is about keeping a firm focus, being able to dominate the mind not only in a particular moment or from time to time, but for a long time. The normal state of mind should be one of concentration. When we start climbing, either because we don't have much practice yet or simply because we just got on the rock and are still warming up, concentration comes and goes. We must be attentive and refocus if an intrusive thought creeps in and may cause fear or distraction. However, climbing can also become meditation when we are able to maintain this concentration —in fact, many people already feel this way. That is, when we do not struggle to eliminate thoughts or get caught up in them —our mind is clear. No distractions or fluctuations, no projections. Just flowing through the rock, precisely executing the movements and even intuitively finding the holds.

The moves may be easy or difficult, the rock may be pointy and your hands may be bleeding, or there may be a lot of fuss at the foot of the route. You may not even know the next sequence of moves. But this doesn't create doubt or insecurity. You are absorbed in your climbing. You and the rock, no irrational fears, no intrusive thoughts about what you are going to do next or what you forgot to do. All mental processes have stopped. There is surrender, there is present, there is focus. And you enjoy it. At this moment climbing is much more than balance in motion. It is stillness in movement, it is peace of mind, it is *Samadhi*.

Samadhi

When the climber's consciousness merges with his climbing and is able to transcend himself, the limitations and projections of the ego/mind are left behind and do not get in the way. You can empty yourself of your conditioning and stop projecting it onto the rock. You fully merge with the experience.

> 3.3 When consciousness is absorbed in its purpose, it is in deep concentration and total integration (*samadhi*).
>
> *Yoga Sutras*, Paranjali

Samadhi is the culmination of the path of yoga. If we get metaphorical, we could say that it is the "sending" of the "route" of yoga. It is the integration of all the previous steps. Just like sending a route is the integration of all the factors (technique, concentration, physical and mental strength, etc.) and necessary movements (the slab step, the final overhang, locking off to reach the undercling, etc.). That is to say, when one has managed to align all of one's capabilities with the demands of the route and has become "one" with it.

Samadhi is something that happens. It cannot be

forced, nor can it be practiced, but it is the result of all the other steps above, just as it is the result of sending a route. You practice the necessary movements, you train or learn what you must until you reach the point where the route is sent.

In *samadhi*, also interpreted as final union or total integration, you transcend the dualities of the ego (yes or no, good or bad, easy or difficult, etc.), dissolving all boundaries and integrating fully into the experience, into the purpose. If you are climbing, you will feel you are one with the rock, your mind will not be fragmented or sow doubts about which grip to hold or whether a foothold is better or worse. Your mind will simply use efficiently whatever it has at its disposal —be it the smallest crimp or the farthest edge— flowing along the wall as if it were the extension of oneself.

In yoga, several types of *samadhi* are differentiated. The main ones are *samadhi* with seed (*savikalpa samadhi*) and seedless *samadhi* (*nirvikalpa samadhi*). In *samadhi* with seed, a transitory *samadhi* is experienced, as there remain parts of the ego that re-germinate —fears, desires, attachments, aversions, etc. Continuing with the metaphor, you could say that you sent the route, but when you try it again another day you find that you are still afraid of the complicated steps and your mind is still churning when you climb it. Or it could be the "little *samadhis*" that you gain along the way. These "revelations" allow you to decipher each step of the route, one by one, although you have not fully integrated them yet.

Seedless *samadhi* is a state of abiding, where you have truly freed yourself from conditioning and projections. You have definitely "sent" the route and transcended the fears you felt in some steps. They no longer distress you, limit you, nor enslave you. In this seedless *samadhi*, those fears and/or conditioning in general were eradicated in the process, so they do not germinate again, that is, you do not take them with you to the next route. They don't manifest themselves again, so this is something that you take with you everywhere, into your whole life, into everything you do. Just to give an example, the ability to manage discomfort and stay calm that you develop by climbing and that you can take with you and apply it in any other area. It can also be thought of as when you get a hold of a grade and now all the routes marked with that little number seem easy, you flow through them at a glance, without questioning the difficulty of the steps. Despite how hard it was to climb this grade at the time, the demands of these routes are so integrated into your repertoire now that you can climb them in deep concentration, nothing standing between your mind and the rock.

Remember that we are still in the realm of simile and metaphor, for *samadhi* is an experience so profound, so encompassing and so personal that not even the great yogis have ventured to describe it in words.

In fact, in seedless *samadhi* we do not even need to concentrate on something to experience it.

So much for the development of the eight limbs of yoga. We will now delve deeper into some concepts that may be useful in this exploration of yoga.

Samyama

Samyama is the application of the last three steps (*dharana, dhyana* and *samadhi*) to either an object, idea or practice. By applying this deep concentration on something, one can gain deep and superior knowledge about the object.

> 3.5 When *samyama* is mastered, the light of knowledge appears.
>
> *Yoga Sutras*, Paranjali

From the practice of *samyama* come the *siddhis*, the results of the practice of yoga. These are the so-called supernatural powers of the yogis. These powers seem impossible to us to attain and are therefore the part of the yoga sutras that are most difficult for our minds to assimilate. In the last sutras of the third chapter, Patanjali lists some of these powers such as the ability to enter another body, to regulate hunger and thirst at will or to gain unbreakable strength, among others.

In order to better understand *samyama* and its application without the mind hindering us with its objections, let us take the example of climbing, as we have been doing throughout this book.

If we apply *samyama* to a route we want to climb, concentrating on it, meditating on and during the climb and reaching some *samadhis* (revelations or small moments of enlightenment), we will realize that we are also acquiring powers, achieving things that seemed impossible before. That is, we get to know the secrets of the route, we discover the right combination, the hidden truth, the "tricks" that we can apply —the best grips, where to hold them from, the correct position of the feet, the rests and the best posture to take advantage of them, etc.

Remember the first few times you climb a project, a route that is somewhat above your grade. You don't move, it seems impossible. It is beyond your mind that climbing it is even a possibility for you. However, you concentrate on the route, you try it several times, you let a few days go by (although you still have the movements in mind, repeating them in your head on a loop). You go back to the route, you concentrate, you observe the rock or how other people move on it, you try different combinations, remove your mental barriers, fight your fears... You can break down each of these processes and apply *samyama* to each of them gradually.

> 3.6 The application of *samyama* is gradual.
>
> *Yoga Sutras*, Paranjali

A good example of the gradual application of *samyama*

is when there is a movement of the route that does not work for us, and we repeat it several times until we figure out how to perform it. In other words, we apply *samyama* until the path is illuminated, we discover the combination needed to perform the step, learning to discriminate which grips to take and which not to take, which sequences are possible, and which are impossible, among other things. Let us see how this process is described in the sutras:

> 3.53 By *samyama* over each moment of a sequence comes the knowledge born from right discrimination (viveka).
>
> *Yoga Sutras*, Paranjali

The discriminative capacity (*viveka*) is one of the most important capabilities to cultivate on the path of yoga. It enables us to differentiate the real from the illusory, to discern what leads us on the path from what leads us astray, what brings us peace of mind from what brings us agitation. Differentiating the holds and rests that work for us and those that don't. Also discriminating the moments when our mind makes us believe we can't from the situations when we really can't, among many other examples you can think of on how to discriminate based on a criterion.

Sending a route is a complex process, but, in essence, it consists of concentrating deeply on the route or on each of the separate parts and not giving up, persisting in *samyama* (concentration, meditation, *samadhi*). Then, little by little, the necessary skills — the powers— come to you: the knowledge of the technique you lacked, the right sequence discarding the wrong one, or developing the strength you needed, among other things that the route demanded.

After all, how do you achieve superhuman feats in climbing, such as great climbs or legendary ascents? Through deep concentration on these objectives, as simple as that, as difficult as that. The yogis called this process *Samyama* and the great feats or powers *siddhis*.

While these powers come when we have succeeded in removing some of the obstacles of mental fluctuations, Patanjali cautions us against becoming distracted or ego-filled by the attainment of the powers and encourages us to follow the path toward total liberation from the fluctuations of the mind.

> 3.38 The powers derived from *samyama* may seem like extraordinary attainments, but they hinder *samadhi* if they distract us from total integration.
>
> *Yoga Sutras*, Paranjali

In other words, to continue our simile, don't get attached to the grade or the route you have sent and keep on working. Don't settle, keep moving toward your purpose. Keep walking your *sadhana*.

Sadhana

To end this part of the book, I would like to go back to the beginning. This last chapter is a kind of call to action to set out on your own path, your own *sadhana*, now with the perspective that I hope you gained through the journey of yoga and climbing from this book.

Sadhana translates as spiritual path. Everyone has their own and can choose to walk it in different ways. But that is the main requirement, to walk it. It is something to focus on, it does not just happen. You must journey through it; it doesn't come looking for you. It is more a duty than a right. The ability to maintain equanimity or the famous "enlightenment", like anything else we want to achieve, is not something that happens by divine command, nor is it a birthright of a privileged few. There is no miracle pill or magic recipe to achieve it. This way of thinking is just an excuse for our ego to perpetuate itself and not get the job done.

Climbing can be one of the many means at our disposal to traverse this path. Furthermore, it is important to be clear that it is only a means to an end, just like the different types of yoga that have been developed over thousands of years. Keep in mind that we must look at the moon, not at the finger pointing to it. That is, look toward the supreme purpose to which they point to without getting too distracted by the form. This purpose is the attainment of peace of mind, the stilling of the mind, as Patanjali indicates at the beginning of the yoga sutras and as other philosophies such as Stoicism or Taoism —explored earlier in this series—, also proclaim. Climbing, as it is proposed in these books, can be a prism through which to look, a microscope through which to analyze yoga (or other philosophical currents). However, we should not over-identify with the lens.

Just as this path can be journeyed on the rock, it can be extrapolated to all your life and traversed at any time and in any place. Suffering and obstacles caused by the human mind manifest everywhere, so the path that leads to liberation from suffering must be traveled if you want to transcend and stop being a puppet shaken by the mind strings. Although we know the eight limbs of yoga to master our mind, it is also important to know in depth why we must master our mind, as I advanced in the first chapters. Now, after what we have gone through during the previous pages, we can dive deeper into this idea, so that all the pieces fit together better.

Our mind puts obstacles in our way because it does not perceive things as they are, but it tints the perceptions, modifying reality. These are the conditionings that have been mentioned so much throughout the book and that are the root of suffering. They are the obstacles that our mind projects and prevent us from achieving calm, happiness or, in general, any goal we set for ourselves —like sending a route. In yoga, these dyes that color our perceptions are called *kleshas*. There are five types of *kleshas*.

The first —and main one, from which the rest are born— is *avidya*, the ignorance of the causes, of the nature of things and of the relation that our mind and its projections have with them. Ignorance of the laws to which the events obey and, therefore, everything that happens to us. As it cannot be otherwise, let's see it with a climbing example. If I constantly fall on the same point of the route, it is most likely that this has a cause, although I do not know it. Whether it's that I'm getting my holds wrong, that I need to bring my feet higher up, or that I'm not even finding the right holds, there is a cause or set of causes that inevitably cause me to fail until I discover the cause and modify my behavior. We tend to easily see the consequence but ignore the cause —which is usually our own mind/ego with its preconceived ideas and projections. This ignorance of the cause (and our role in it) is *avidya*.

The second, *asmita*, is the identification with the ego, with the mind. We believe in our mental projections too much. We believe that we are the one who climbs badly or well, who is afraid or who is good at overhangs; the one who knows how to solve a step but is bad at the next one, who climbs a certain grade and who, if a route is of a higher level, finds it impossible, or if it is a lower level, does not allow himself to try it, even if it is a nice route. And so on and so forth. We take the role we play too seriously, even if it has the worst effects on our life, even if we are missing out on great things just by keeping ourselves sheltered under our ego-disguise.

The third of these obstacles, *raga*, is attachment, which is the addiction to pleasure. Attachment is an obstacle in that it limits and conditions our life. If I am too attached to the comfort of binge-watching shows on the couch, I will hardly find the time and desire to climb. If I am attached to slab climbing or any other type of rock, I will hardly want to expose myself to something different, even though if I do, the growth will be much greater than if I stick to what I am good at and what gives me pleasure. We tend to believe that happiness is the constant search for pleasure —and no wonder, since this is the story that has always been sold to us. But if we stop to think about it, what gave us more satisfaction: sending that route that cost us so much or eating that delicious meal? I know, they can't be compared, but what I think is clear is that the comfortable and hedonistic life is not always (or rather almost never) a happy life. It is rather boring and meaningless. Anyway, both sending the route and eating are some kind of pleasure. They are just examples. What yoga and its path are all about is detachment from both pleasure and aversion, since happiness is already within us, and these are just obstacles that trap our mind and distract us from manifesting it.

And here comes the other part, *dvesha*, aversion, which is the association of something with pain. You probably have an aversion to that route that you have such a hard time with and from which you have fallen off several times. That type of rock, those holds that you don't know how to grab or those steps that you're afraid of, that's aversion. Both things, pleasure and aversion are obstacles to our spiritual path, to achieve our purpose, or to send a route. The *sadhaka* (person who walks the *sadhana*) aspires to peace of mind in any situation, to equanimity. Therefore, they must be above attachment and aversion. They must transcend the two poles for his path to be holistic.

It is not possible to walk the spiritual path only on good vibes from the yoga class, from walking in the mountains or drinking beers with friends, and then at the slightest difficulty —on the rock, at work, on the mat or with another person— we lose our calm and let our mind jump around like an angry monkey, keeping us in unhappiness. Just like the climber who wants to send a route, we must go through both the beautiful and enjoyable passages where we sing along, as well as through the scarcest part of the slab or the most challenging overhang.

The route is the route, *sadhana* is all encompassing and we cannot go about clinging to the part we like and avoiding the other. This way no route is sent and no progress is made in stopping mental fluctuations.

The last of these obstacles is *abhinivesha* —clinging to life, the fear of death. Here Patanjali is more lenient, as he considers it the most difficult to overcome, difficult even for the wisest. The background to this is that, in the Hindu context, death is just another change, a departure, a transition to another life, so it is not to be feared. To understand it a little better, we can interpret it as the fear of loss, the fear of change. To continue talking about departures, we can use the example of having to move for work reasons. Surely, we find it hard to let go of our house, our friends and climbing partners, or our favorite climbing sector. But how can you know that this is a loss? Maybe where you're moving to isn't as big a house as the one you had, but the views are nicer. Maybe you can make great new friends to complement the ones you already have. You might even discover new climbing sectors that are a little different from what you're used to and that leads you to work on your fears and weaknesses.

Now that you know the five obstacles, it is worth repeating that they are the causes that condition our whole life and cause all manifestations (results). This is the concept of *karma*. Our actions, tinged with any of these five *kleshas*, cause a series of reactions that are the reality in which we live. Again, so simple, so difficult. Imagine you are climbing a route and you find yourself with two holds: a sparce crimp in the middle of the route, or a good hold but it deviates quite a bit from the route. If, because of your aversion to the crimp and your attachment to comfort, you deviate to take the good hold, this action will have its consequences, such as you having to make unnatural moves or finding it difficult to return to the original line of the route, even moving away from the bolts. You will fall or be more afraid than you would have been if you had not let yourself be carried away by your ego that preferred the easy way to the right way.

So, going back to the beginning, to overcome these causes and stop these projections of the mind that create *karma* or reactions and disturb the peace of our true self, Patanjali proposes we walk the path of the eight limbs laid out in the body of this book. He also gives us two guidelines we can follow to walk this path: practice (*abhyasa*) and detachment (*vairagya*).

Do not be satisfied with intellection. Don't just read this book, put it into practice. That is what it has been written for, uniting the teachings of yoga with the practical experience of climbing. *Abhyasa* means that one must choose to make the effort to walk the path, one's own *sadhana* that leads to peace of mind. Like any practice, it must be sustained over time, it is not something you do once in a while. In climbing, just as in anything else, if you only practice it once every two months you will hardly make progress and you will be starting from scratch every time you do it.

> 1.14 Practice becomes firmly rooted when it is sustained over time, without interruption and with dedication.
>
> Yoga Sutras, Paranjali

If practice is what needs to be done, the other part is what to stop doing. *Vairagya* is to let go of attachment to things that limit us. Emptying ourselves of what does not serve us in order to fill ourselves with what does (and practice it). For this it is quite useful and important to develop the discriminative capacity (*viveka*) that we talked about in the previous chapter. The ability to discern between what to do and what to let go of, which is not always the same for everyone and changes over different situations or stages of our life. As examples we can say that we should climb what we like or what serves us and detach ourselves from our fear. Work on what we know we must work on and detach ourselves from comforts and the fear of losing them. To walk our *sadhana* and detach from the things that keep us repeating patterns and mental projections. To walk our own path of climbing and detach from both the overindulgence of always staying below our potential and comparing ourselves to others or chasing external achievements, such as grades or collecting routes. Achievements and great climbs can be a consequence of walking your path, as well as another obstacle you must transcend in order to stop feeding your ego.

> "Mountains are not stadiums where I satisfy my ambition to achieve, they are the cathedrals where I practice my religion."
>
> Anatoli Bukréyev.

PARTE II
Swami Climbananda

Peter, the Sadhaka

After various vagaries of life and intense spiritual searches in the most diverse philosophical currents of the world, Peter had found his place in this secluded ashram[4]. He spent his days deepening in yoga, alongside his companions, masters and nature. He felt that only in this environment could he develop the necessary will to make significant progress on the arduous path to meet the Self.

It had now been three years since he had joined them, and indeed, his progress had been significant. When he first arrived, the few answers he had managed to find had been of little use to him in the face of the disturbances of his mind and its projections, which caused him to live in a continuous state of unease and unbearable existential discomfort. However, during his time in the ashram, thanks to yoga, its methods, and the discipline with which he practiced, he had managed to make his mind an ally. Maybe some days his mind was a bit more unruly and tormented him a little, but he was fully aware that the

---

[4] Similar to a monastery, it is a place of meditation and teaching of some of the Hindu currents in which students live under the same roof as their masters.

path is long and, as far as he knew he was going in the right direction, he didn't need to hurry. He had found his place.

Routine had made the days go by at a good pace. The deep study of the texts, exercise of *asanas*, *pranayamas*, meditations, talks with companions and masters or the daily tasks had kept him deeply concentrated in his sadhana. Being in a remote natural setting, the only possible "distraction" was the observation of nature, a very interesting activity for anyone who wants to know themselves.

But something was disturbing the small microcosm surrounding the ashram. A short distance behind it was a large rock face that, with the rise in popularity of climbing, had piqued the interest of the local community. Gradually the flow of people through the area increased significantly. It was not disturbing to the peace of the place, but the trail that ran alongside the ashram began to be traveled at least a couple of times a day, somewhat more on weekends.

This did not disturb the inhabitants of the ashram at all. For them it was simply a kind of concentration exercise, an opportunity to strengthen their ability to persist, to stick to what they were doing, without being influenced by external stimuli. They did not let their minds be distracted by the conversations of the hikers on the trail below the windows. They did not devote any effort to watching who was going up the mountain, when and how. It was enough for them to watch their own minds and attend to their routines and tasks.

Contact between climbers and yogis was reduced to a wave of the hand or a couple of words as a greeting when they passed each other in the vicinity. However, Peter's curiosity began to awake. His mind was still focused on his own things, but he seemed a little more permeable to these external stimuli than his companions. Maybe the window of his room being one of the few that faced the rock wall directly might have had something to do with it, and sometimes he could not help but watch the climbers who were ascending it. These glances, which at first were just diversions from his tasks, gradually turned into contemplation, into a kind of meditation. It became no different from watching the birds or the flow of a river. Some of his companions did not understand what aroused his interest and even felt pity for him, as if he had become distracted from his path, yielding to the whims of the mind. The truth was that his own master had advised him to engage in these contemplative practices. He reassured him by pointing out that it was unnecessary to repress himself, that it was much better to accept this tendency of his mind and observe his reactions. This would lead him to know himself better and to explore this path until little by little the mind could be redirected back to the inner path.

Indeed, as the days went by, he was significantly

reducing his contemplations of the rock and its climbers. Little by little he was letting go of that impulse of the mind toward the contemplation of the different, of the external. However, his interest in the subject remained latent and there were still many unknowns that his mind had yet to resolve. Why did they do it? Was it some kind of meditation or just an ego impulse? Did they get satisfaction from doing the activity itself or were they looking for some result?

These questions piled up in his head from time to time, but he made it his conscious job not to get too caught up in them and not to let them distract him from his daily practices and routines.

The opportunity

One day, after a sunny morning, the sky suddenly darkened. Large storm clouds gathered overhead and in a matter of minutes a heavy rainstorm broke out. This caught by surprise not only the aspiring yogis, who were doing their chores in the surrounding area, but also a couple of groups of climbers who were descending the trail back down from the rock. This trail was usually not difficult or dangerous, but when it rained, large puddles would form and everything would get muddy. Moving along it became a difficult exercise in stealth and steadiness. What was an easy trail under normal conditions, could now become a slide down the steep mountainside. The ashram's yoga students were aware of this, so as soon as they realized that people were still walking down the path, they were quick to step out to warn of the situation.

There were only two female climbers still coming down the path with their large backpacks filled with climbing gear. The rain was pouring down, and when they passed the yogis' windows, these invited them to rest inside and wait for the rain to ease a bit before continuing on their way back, since they still had a couple of sections where they would have to walk very carefully. They accepted the invitation, went inside and were served tea.

Peter clearly identified the opportunity. While his companions, indifferent, continued with their tasks, he approached them and asked them all sorts of questions about climbing. Questions that had been on his mind for weeks. Some were answered, others were not so easy to respond to. Seeing his great curiosity about the subject, the climbers told him that the best way to find out the answers he was looking for was to try it out for himself. They invited him to accompany them to the wall on their next outing, which would be in a couple of days, when the rock was again dry and in good condition. He accepted, shyly but impulsively, and they agreed that they would pick him up in a few days.

Doubts

In the days following this visit, he pondered the question: would he be giving in to the worldly impulses of his mind? Would it be dangerous? Would he be wasting his energies doing activities that were not part of his routine? Was he straying away from his path? These questions disturbed his peace of mind quite a lot. He found it difficult to concentrate on his meditations and became clumsier in carrying out his daily tasks. He was not the only one with these fears in his mind. He could also see them reflected in his companions whenever he approached them to ask for their opinion. Some were happy for him and supportive, happy that he dared to do such a thing and hoped that he would tell them about his adventure when he returned. Others, however, though they were as careful as possible to refrain from expressing or showing their disapproval, could not entirely conceal what they thought: deep down they felt that he was indulging in the impulses and desires of the mind. They considered it an absurd pastime, a passing fad among the Sunday-trippers.

In the midst of such mental tribulations, Peter did not want to make a big deal about it to his masters. The latter, like the good yogis they were, knew about the question as they were very good observers and what went on around them was never a secret to them, not even the minds of their students. But their stance on the matter was clear; they were equanimous on the issue and did not judge the student's decisions. They knew that it was all part of life and the path to be travelled, which is different for everyone. They also knew that self-experimentation is the best way to go down any path. They simply let it be what it had to be, without repressing or encouraging, without interfering in the matter.

ROCK DAY

When the day agreed upon for rock climbing arrived, the climbers passed by the ashram on their way to the wall. Peter, who rose at dawn and deployed all the resources he had to calm and quiet the mind (*asanas*, *pranayamas*, meditation...), finally felt at peace with his decision and was ready to accompany them on such an interesting experience. It would be hard to tell who was more fascinated about the other: the climbers about the yogi or the yogi about the climbers.

They reached the wall, which was even more imposing up close than from his window. Again, he was assailed by all sorts of doubts, fears and dispersions at the sight of heights and difficulties. He was concentrating on being a mere observer of these things that haunted his head, but he could not help but be somewhat dismayed by these travails of his mind. The climbers noticed his concerns despite the efforts he made to conceal them and they patiently explained to him all the basics of the activity and the material used, thus managing to relax him a little.

They started on the visibly easier routes on the wall. The "warm-up" routes, as they called them.

Seeing them climb so smoothly and seeing that they could enjoy it, he managed to relax his remaining tension away.

They lent him their harness and climbing shoes, and strung him up. He began to climb up the route, imitating some of the moves he had previously seen. He was getting impressively good at it. His body, strong and flexible thanks to the *asanas* he is used to practice, was responding perfectly to the physical demands of the activity. The heights did not faze him either, as he was able to verify for himself the safety of the rope and equipment right from the start of the route. When he came down, he was overcome with immense joy and satisfaction. He could not believe that he had been able to climb and, moreover, that he could have enjoyed it in this way. He kept showing his gratitude to his "mentors", who were happy to see his reaction. However, it didn't take long for them to pick up the equipment and move a few meters down the foot of the wall to look for their next objective, the next route to climb.

The Challenge

His companions began to climb a visibly more difficult route, with smaller holds and more complicated or physically demanding moves. Peter felt confident after the first experience, he felt he could encounter difficulty, but, at the same time, he saw himself capable of managing it. When it was his turn and he was offered to try it, he didn't think too much about it. He wanted to experience the previous sensations again.

He was warned that the route was more difficult, and that he should take it easy in the face of this physical and mental challenge.

He, who considered that he had great mastery over his mind thanks to his path in yoga, along with a great physical condition, eagerly went to the wall to relive that experience.

He began to climb the route. Everything was going smoothly well. The moves were demanding but manageable. Then, toward the upper half of the route, the hand and foot holds began to be more limited, small or difficult to find. And he fell. He didn't hurt himself, but it was a strange feeling for him, it was uncomfortable. He tried again, but now he was flooded with doubt and fear. His mind was out of control. He began to doubt his abilities and the material. He wondered what he was doing hanging there instead of following his routine of spiritual realization. These doubts prevented him from correctly executing the movements. The fear of falling again made his body tense and he did not grasp the grips with the necessary confidence. He could not relax, his mind kept projecting all kinds of negative thoughts and emotions. He could not concentrate on what he was doing. He had to descend without finishing the route, without reaching the top.

When he reached the ground, he was visibly disturbed and confused. His companions tried to encourage him, affirming that what he had felt was perfectly normal and that the route was substantially difficult for him to overcome it easily on his first day.

He was not really confused and disturbed by his performance on the route, but by the reaction of his mind to the event itself, by the mental whirlwinds experienced in what he thought was his equanimous mind. It seemed as if all the path he so strictly traversed had been for nothing. He felt devastated.

He apologized to his companions and moved a little aside from the group to sit down to try to dissolve the whirlwinds and calm his mind to think clearly again. He thought that, thanks to yoga, he had already achieved a high level of mastery over his mind. He knew for a fact that he still had a long way to go, but he could not imagine that an activity like rock climbing could be so disturbing to him. He was so distressed that he could not even see himself able to return to the ashram. How could he present himself to his companions and masters with such a scattered mind? How could he be able to explain such a setback on his path to equanimity? It was not a matter of pride or shame, he simply needed answers to the whole series of new unknowns that were being posed to him. He needed to keep climbing. He needed to keep experiencing those sensations, both good and bad, to get to know himself better and see if he was really capable of mastering his mind in those kinds of situations as well. He went back to the climbers as they were finishing their climb. He was calmer, but still anxious about his thoughts. They chatted for a while as they gathered the gear, and in the course of the conversation he discovered that climbing routes have names. The route that had been his turning point was called "Dharma". This circus that is the world has a great sense of humor. This was quite a sign to do what he was thinking of doing: he would stay on the wall until he was able to really master his mind. He wrote a short note for the climbers to hand to one of his ashram companions on their way down and sought refuge in a cavity in the wall. The climbers, concerned, offered him some of the clothes they were wearing and other things that might be useful to him. However, he was already quite accustomed to austerities, so this situation did not seem to him to be a great discomfort.

THE DARK NIGHT

The night was dark, both in the sky and in his mind. After seeing how vulnerable he was still to the fluctuations of the mind and its games, he felt a deep anguish, rooted in all kinds of fears and doubts about his existence and the path he had taken. How could it be that after years of intense practice he could fall back into such mental whirlwinds? How could he not even quiet his mind now? He wanted to meditate and silence those thoughts, but he could not concentrate. His mind jumped from one thought to another, he seemed to have lost all the mastery he thought he had. There were very low moments when he even doubted the teachings he had received. His mind was taking him to darker and darker places, so he decided to leave the cave (literally and metaphorically). He went for a walk, hoping that moving his body a little would help him quiet his mind or, at least, get it out of the loop of harmful thoughts in which it was stuck. And it worked. His mind gave him a truce. He took advantage of that space to bring his mind back to sadhana. He remembered one of his favorite sutras that had been very helpful to him on previous occasions:

> 2.33 Negative thoughts can be neutralized by cultivating the opposite thoughts.

THE REVELATION

From concentrating on this simple sutra he found the tip from which to unravel the tangled skein. Instead of questioning himself and his sadhana, he decided to focus on finding a way to adapt what he already knew to the new situation. Instead of letting his mind dwell on the limits he had just discovered, the difficulties he might encounter, or the negatives of the experience in general, he decided to focus on how yoga could help him overcome this challenge, how he could use this experience to continue to grow, to walk his path. He finally managed to stop the flow of negative thoughts and his mind found rest. From this revelation and the mental clarity it brought him, he came to the conclusion that, yoga being a method of mastering the mind, he would just have to apply it consciously to overcome the challenges posed by this new adventure, climbing, which was no different from any other activity in life.

He didn't quite know where to begin to apply the yoga method. This was a very different activity from what he was used to. He missed being able to consult his masters and companions, who were only a few hundred meters down the mountain. However, he was able to quickly detach himself from this mental impulse, as he himself had studied and memorized the scriptures. Thus, the question was how to find his own way to apply them to this unfamiliar experience, but not so different from any other experience of the world and the human mind.

KRIYA YOGA

He meditated deeply on the scriptures, reciting the Yoga Sutras, staying absorbed in them, until the solution to how to start this new path revealed itself. Moreover, it was the most obvious one. The beginning of the chapter on the path (*Sadhana Pada*) would serve to start him on his climbing path. In the first sutra of this chapter, Patanjali sets out the parts that make up *Kriya Yoga* or yoga of practice. These are

Tapas, Svadhyaya and *Ishvarapranidhana*.

Throughout the next few days, he kept these three key points in his mind as he climbed. He met several people climbing different routes of different levels and with different approaches. Some enjoyed trying different routes while others repeated the same routes over and over again. Some talked about grades, sport achievements and sending routes, while others climbed more recreationally, for relaxation or for new experiences. Peter concentrated on sharing as many experiences as possible, while observing the reactions of his own mind. When it projected an obstacle, when something caused him pleasure or aversion, when fear and frustration set in, or when an experience was satisfying. He was attentive to everything that happened both inside and outside his mind. This continuous observation of himself and others was part of his practice of *Svadhyaya*. This practice consists of the study of oneself, or rather of the Self —of which the scriptures that inspired his practice (the Yoga Sutras) speak of—, the divine essence in all of us, what remains when we eliminate the mind and its conditioning.

For his study to be successful it was necessary to take it beyond the limits of the ego, so the practice of *Tapas* was something that had to be present at the same time. He must have the discipline to go beyond self-imposed limits. In his case, and as an example, he had to transcend his shyness to establish contact with the people who frequented the climbing wall. He had to try routes of different grades and styles, subjugate the ego that wanted to avoid the sections of the wall that seemed more complicated or not let the falls condition or limit his progress. If in order to carry out a rigorous self-study in climbing he had to maintain a high level of attention and concentration, this also served him to find ways to cultivate that discipline. Discipline that would burn away the fears, limits and aversions that his mind, his lower self, wanted him to continually project. As soon as he was distracted or his mind wandered, he would find his mind filled again with excuses, fears of heights, the desire to return to his stay in the ashram, doubts about his progress or insecurities about whether the chosen path was worth it, among many other thoughts that he had to be aware of in order to redirect himself to his purpose.

He found the strength he needed for this in the third pillar of *Kriya Yoga, Ishvarapranidhana*. Surrender to something higher, as is the path of yoga. Devotion to the process, detachment from the results, moving unconditionally toward his purpose, surrendering to whatever teachings the climb or anything else on his path brought him. Regardless of whether it was, for example, a frustration resulting from not being able to get a single step on the route or, on the contrary, the celebration, together with other people, of a good send.

These practices served to bring himself and his yoga practice into climbing. It should be said that, although kriya yoga makes up only the last three parts of *niyama*, he remained compliant with the rest of the *niyamas*, as well as the yamas, throughout his practice as an intrinsic part of his way of being. This also allowed his daily life on the wall to be a joyful experience. With his gentle attitude and a settled non-harming (ahimsa) attitude, he won the sympathy of both the climbers and other people who hiked in the surrounding area. Even the birds, who, detecting no hostility in him, continued to go about their daily routines in his presence and even occasionally shared food with him. In a few days he became a beloved member of the local climbing community who frequently came to the wall. Without being intrusive, without forcing his way or coveting gear or ropes, he was invited to share climbs with everyone who went to the crag, even being provided with all the necessary gear, without asking for anything in return. He was content with what came to him and, therefore, what he needed always came to him.

Asana

When his practice had settled down, he considered further advancement in the method of yoga. The next step was *Asana*. It was obvious that his previous *asana* practice had provided him with a strong and flexible physique that was a good base for climbing, but even so climbing was still something totally different from how he was used to use his body. At first, he tried practicing *asanas* that might make it easier for him to perform the movements he wanted to execute on the wall. This proved useful for a bit, but the amount of different movements that are needed when climbing a wall are very difficult to replicate and required improvisation and a flexible mind that could integrate new postures on each type of rock, in each sequence. Instinctively he knew that there would be some way to transcend the yoga *asana* concept programmed in his mind to adapt it to his new path. Meditating again on the Yoga Sutras, he realized that the basic concept of *asana* could be perfectly applicable to climbing. According to his interpretation of Patanjali's sutras, the *asana* must be a firm and comfortable posture, which is achieved when you manage to relax in it, transcending dualities (comfortable-uncomfortable, good-bad, etc.). Thus, an *asana* can be any posture on the wall as long as it is possible to maintain both firmness and comfort. A posture that is solid but soft at the same time. Stable but relaxed. The more he practiced a route the more he found his "*asanas*" within it. What climbers called natural rests, he saw it as an opportunity to practice his *asanas*. He would look for a posture that he could hold firmly, whether it was catching a good edge, locking a knee, spreading his legs between two walls, or positioning his body close to the wall on a ledge. It all depended on the possibilities the wall offered.

From his previous yoga *asana* practices, he had acquired great naturalness in the mastery of *bandhas*, the application of which he found interesting in this new *asana* experience. *Bandhas* are controlled and sustained muscular contractions that serve as energetic locks, a strategic activation of certain muscles to concentrate strength and create stability. He found it particularly useful to experiment with using *mula bandha* (pelvic floor contraction) to stabilize the body and keep it close to the wall, while creating a sense of lightness. *Pada bandha* allowed him to block the energy of the foot by consciously applying force, so that the foot became an active grip. Locked in its rock foothold or inside the climbing shoe, it relieved the tension of the rest of the muscles and body parts. Instead, if he simply rested the foot on the rock without applying the energetic block, the force would be dispersed throughout the rest of the body parts without being firmly established.

The same thing happened with *Hasta bandha*, the energetic lock of the hand, which was of great help in the rests where he had to rest his hands or grasp parts of the rock that were blunt, flat or slopers, among others. The combination of these blocks, performed without forcing, allowed him to correctly channel the energy to the points that needed it most. He thus concentrated his forces and generated firmness and stability while avoiding the dispersion of his energy through other parts. For example, he used this hand lock instead of blocking only from the arm or shoulder muscles, which were less efficient at keeping the body where he wanted to keep it.

Once he found the position he could hold firmly, he took the time to settle into it, to make it comfortable. He practiced again and again until he was able to soften his mind. In this way he managed to take his attention away from the discomfort and difficulties, concentrating on infinity instead of on the details of the small muscular discomforts he might be feeling in such unusual positions held in the middle of a wall. When he managed to transcend the dialogue projected by his mind (this grip is not good for resting, this foot is not very stable, my muscles are straining, among others...), he knew that he had mastered that *asana* or rest. The position that at first seemed to be a pain and sapped his energy had become his ally now that he had expanded his ability to be comfortable in the uncomfortable. He worked to improve his rock *asanas* so that they would allow him to efficiently tackle the next steps of the route, which could be seen as transitions between *asanas*. These sequences also required great mastery of the body and mind, to be able to maintain concentration and precisely execute the movements, so the next yoga step could be key: *Pranayama*.

Pranayama

He had practiced countless *pranayama* exercises and knew well of its powerful and immediate effects on the mind and energy. Now he wanted to figure out how he could use it on the rock. It was impossible for him to even try to control his breathing when he was performing complicated movements. But when he managed to settle into a rest/*asana*, he found the perfect opportunity to practice and experiment. Normally, because the climb was demanding, he would reach these rests with his heart pounding, his breathing racing, and his mind starting to wander. The mind would try to project doubts and insecurities so that he would stop climbing, so that he could not transcend the limits he had set for himself. This was the ideal moment to practice *pranayama*. Through different techniques that included different ways of prolonging his inhalations, retentions and exhalations, bringing his attention to the different points of the process and performing a variable number of them, he achieved immediate effects on his mind, which started to calm down. When he reached the *asana* after a couple of hard movements, he was exhausted, and his mind began to project doubts about his own capacity or fears about the distance to the next bolt. But, after a few consciously expanded breaths, he managed to bring his mind back to the calm state needed to concentrate again and see things clearly for what they were. His heart regained a steady, leisurely rhythm and his energies were renewed to allow him to face the next challenges the route had in store. Although he was already familiar with the use of *pranayama*, using it in climbing was a great revelation to him. Never before had he used it in a situation of such physical and mental agitation, so he was able to see firsthand the great effect that breathing has on mental states, body and energies.

Pratyahara

He was starting to get into the concentration needed to climb efficiently. However, there were still things he was not comfortable with. One of them was the use of climbing shoes. Although he had had occasion to borrow and try different sizes and models, for someone who had spent the last years of his life barefoot or in sandals, he found these shoes absurdly uncomfortable. In addition, after several days of climbing, his hands were full of wounds, calluses and peeled off skin. These issues were getting in the way of his concentration on the routes. He was losing himself by resting in a foothold too thin and feeling the pressure of the shoe on his toes or when he grabbed an edge that just poked at the exact spot where his open wound was. Then it dawned on him that his mind was focusing too much on those things and he was being complicit in it. He remembered the next step he had to apply: *Pratyahara*, the withdrawal of the senses. He was more than used to keeping his hearing or sight from causing his mind to engage with the external while studying or meditating, or even ignoring minor discomforts that arose while sitting in meditation, but he had never had to apply *pratyahara* to a stimulus as strong as the pain his feet felt when they swelled inside his shoes or when he had to apply force to a grip while still having open wounds on his fingers. But any situation can serve to advance in sadhana. That's why he exercised his concentration by focusing on his purpose (climbing the route), directing his mind's attention only to what was aligned with this goal and leaving out any stimuli that were not helpful to the achievement of sending the route. Thus, he could step on a chickpea-sized rock and feel how his toes supported and exerted force at the same time as he could consciously ignore the discomfort of his toes clenched under the rubber shoe. With his fingertips raw he could feel the subtle adhesions of a crack in the wall without being diverted by the pain. With practice and by having his mind directed toward the set purpose, he gained the ability to subtract the senses from unfavorable stimuli, discriminating those that diverted him and attending to those that might further his advancement.

DHARANA

At last, his mind could be directed more or less steadily toward his climbing. After several days of practice and applying the wisdom of yoga to his climbing, he noticed a significant increase in his ability to keep his mind focused on every step he took, every movement of his body, every subtlety of the rock. There were still many moments that pulled him out of this state of concentration. Moments where intrusive thoughts crept in, doubts and fears arose, or his attention was diverted. He took these moments as training. It was almost a game. He would stay alert by watching his mind, and when he saw it wander off the route, he would bring it back lovingly, without frustration, but firmly back to the step he was climbing or to the piece of rock where he was exploring the next hold. At this point, climbing had become a mental workout, a way to sharpen his ability to focus, to sustain his attention on his purpose without being distracted by thoughts or external circumstances. If he could learn to stay focused in such an adverse situation as climbing, with its complicated movements and the fears it triggers in the mind, his ability to concentrate would be strengthened and he would find it much easier to apply it to his subsequent practices or any other task in life.

DHYANA

On some routes, his concentration was continuously maintained and became so deep that it turned into meditation. His attention was completely absorbed by his climbing. He was not only focused on each step he took, but also on everything that went with it. The feel of the rock, his breathing or identifying the holds became not obstacles, but tools that his awareness used to not deviate for a moment from his purpose. Despite his years of practicing and instructing himself in yoga, he had rarely managed to really enter a deep meditative state. Normally, when he sat to meditate, he would remain in deep concentration, although this flow would come and go. The mind kept fluctuating, scattering when he least expected it. Only a few times had he entered into what he could consider meditation, where the mind is shut out and there is no awareness of time, space or even the body itself. Thanks to these few experiences he had had, he could see that, sometimes, he would enter a very similar state while climbing. His concentration on the route became so solid and constant that nothing disturbed him. His body flowed without his mind intervening with thoughts or judgments. Only when he reached the final bolt did he realize that he had entered that state. Like when you awake from sleep and realize that you have been dreaming. He didn't even know how to enter that state, he couldn't force his way into it. He just had to focus on concentrating deeply and that state would come over him. If he looked for it or tried to recreate it, it was elusive, so in climbing he discovered a powerful tool to concentrate on in order to access meditation.

"Dharma", the project

It had been a long time since the route called "Dharma" had shattered his paradigms, since his failed attempt had shaken his mind in such a way as to make him realize how little mastery he had over it. But thanks to the difficulty encountered he was able to realize his weaknesses and gave himself the opportunity to work on them. If that day when he went on the wall for the first time had been a gentle stroll, he would have come down just as he went up. Or worse, with a more inflated ego, with no progress on his path, if not a setback.

Almost without realizing it, he had been applying *samyama* to climbing, combining concentration, meditation, and even some spontaneous revelations that could be considered little *samadhis*. Applying this very intense focus of attention, some of the secrets of climbing that used to take years of practice had been unveiled to him, such as the ability to position the body in such a way as to take advantage of even the smallest grip, the use of the rock adherences, the different ways to effectively place the feet, using the natural sway of the body in dynamic movements, among many other skills that unlocked in his mind and body to become a resourceful climber, one that flows gracefully up the wall rather than a tense body that applies physical force against the rock and gravity, wasting his energy.

He felt ready for his final challenge: to send

"Dharma," the route that had started him on the climbing path and which he considered a sort of culmination. It was a demanding route, yes, but he had already successfully climbed other routes that were considered even more demanding among the local climbing community, so he thought the time might have come to measure all his progress on this route.

When the chosen day arrived, he prepared his mind from dawn. He spent the previous hours mobilizing all the resources at his disposal to empty his mind and maintain serenity, such as the recitation of sutras, yoga *asanas* or sitting in meditation for a long time until people began to arrive who could accompany and belay him in his project.

Once everything was ready to start climbing, he approached the wall and began without further ado. At first it took him a while to concentrate. His mind had placed too many expectations on this route and kept interfering and projecting thoughts, trying to sabotage him. But soon he stopped assuming that concentration was a simple task and got down to "work". He began by concentrating on the rests/rock *asanas*. Thanks to the repertoire he had acquired through practice, he began to rest in places that were previously only transitory steps, that is, he began to regain energy where it was previously consumed. He had acquired a certain mastery of his breathing so that he could regulate it naturally, integrated with his practice and aligned with his purpose of maintaining mental calm in each step, transcending the automatic tendency to agitation that characterizes the mind and breath in this type of challenging situations. He kept his breathing slow and prolonged when he had to face a step that required serenity and all his mental clarity. He combined this stillness with moments when he had to take explosive steps and his breathing was held to favor concentration or had to be speeded up to save a sequence that required strength and vigor.

That day was very hot. In addition, there was a large influx of people climbing the adjoining routes and chatting animatedly at the foot of the route. However, he did not let his senses disperse in these stimuli. His ears were closed, his sight only visualized the next steps, he felt neither hot nor cold, he did not judge whether there was more moisture or less in the feel of the rock. He had simply submitted all his senses and his abilities to the present moment, to the purpose, to doing what he had to do at the right time, without dispersions, judgments or excuses.

The concentration that fluctuated in the first few meters of the route began to settle firmly, progressively constituting a moving meditation. Although it was his first time on the upper half of the route, he executed the movements precisely. As if he knew them, as if the rock were his natural environment, as if the route were part of himself. He was flowing, naturally discovering each move, totally absorbed in the activity when, almost without realizing it, he clipped the final bolt. He had completed the route. All his abilities and skills, all his work, had been aligned toward the achievement of the purpose. All the steps of yoga had brought him to his destination, the masterful union of all the parts of the route, of all the sequences, as well as the elimination of all the obstacles that prevented that union, such as fears, doubts, insecurities, attachments, self-imposed limits or other projections of the mind and ego.

He would not know how to describe the sensation he had had climbing and sending that route, but it must have been something similar to what is known as *Samadhi*. It was difficult for him to recognize this for certain because it is an elusive concept that appeals to a state that cannot be described in words. However, the level of mental absorption he had achieved climbing had been supreme and had undoubtedly been the result of the skillful concatenation of all the yoga parts he had been studying and practicing for years. He did not believe that he had reached a permanent "enlightenment" by climbing the route, but he did consider that he had had an experience in which he had really succeeded in merging his mind with the purpose, so at least he knew that it was possible and that he should continue with his sadhana until he reached a lasting, integral *samadhi* that would extend this supreme union of being to his whole life.

Coming back

After this experience, he felt that his adventure was over. He could leave the cave in the rock that had sheltered him for so long and during such an intense transformation. It was time to return to the ashram and continue his study and practice, now with a broader perspective of the powerful teachings of yoga. He was not going too far away; he was simply returning to his dwelling. But he was returning with a firm resolve to keep climbing as part of his sadhana. He would return from time to time to the wall to keep sanding the rough edges of his mind, to continue the work on subjugating his ego whenever it tried to limit and condition him.

On his return he was welcomed with open arms, as always. As if only a few hours had passed since he left. The only difference was that everyone could not suppress their curiosity to know how his rock climbing experience went. He patiently answered all the questions his companions asked him, trying to relate his experience to the yoga concepts they were already familiar with, so to make it more understandable to the rest of the students.

Peter continued to frequently go to the rock to continue his practice and, inevitably, the interest of the sadhakas to experience this practice, this path, grew. His masters, surprised to see how he had been able to integrate teachings that took most aspirants years of practice, allowed the creation of the climbing branch of the ashram. This resulted in several yoga students, led by Peter, making frequent excursions to the nearby wall to experience new ways of deepening the teachings.

Years passed and what began as one person's impulse became an assiduous and complementary practice to the rest of the yogic practices that constituted the ashram's routine.

Peter, by sharing his experience with others and maintaining his practice over time and with dedication, gained a remarkable mastery over his mind and the methods of yoga. He was named master by his masters, receiving the initiate's name of Swami Climbananda. Swami can be translated as master of himself, one who pushes himself, one who follows his own path, in this case. He found his own path in climbing and pushed himself to walk it. He kept at it while dealing, at the same time, with all the difficulties one encounters when trying to do something different from the established. The suffix —ananda means bliss, joy, fulfillment, or happiness, so Climbananda could be translated as "one who has found fulfillment in climbing."

"Follow your path (dharma), however humble it may be, rather than following that of another, however great it may be. To die following one's own path is life; to live following another's is death."

Bhagavad Gita, 3.35

Glossary

AHIMSA

Non-violence, non-harming, renouncing all hostility.

ASANA

Body posture, position.

ASHRAM

Similar to a monastery, it is a place of meditation and teaching of some of the Hindu currents in which students live under the same roof as their masters.

ASTEYA

Not taking what belongs to others, do not steal.

BANDHA

Controlled and sustained muscular contractions that work as energy locks. Strategic activation of certain muscles to concentrate strength and create stability.

BHAGAVAD GITA

Hindu sacred text where, through the epic story of Arjuna and his conversation with Krishna as an incarnated god, the different aspects of the philosophy of yoga are covered.

Bhakti yoga

Yoga of devotion.

Bolts

Usually referred to a plate and a bolt that are the metal elements fixedly anchored to the wall along sport climbing routes. Placed every few meters, they allow the climber to place his quickdraws and place the rope through them, preventing a fall beyond the last bolt through which the rope has passed.

Brahmacharya

Moderation, regulation of impulses.

Climbing area/crag

Place that has been set up for the practice of climbing. These are climbing areas where the routes are usually equipped with anchors so that climbing can be done in a fairly safe way, focusing on the sportiest part of climbing.

Climbing grades

An element of information consisting of assigning values that grade the difficulty of a route. They serve mainly to help us decide if a climb is within our possibilities or not. The most commonly used grade scales in sport climbing are the American and the French scale, but there are many more.

CLIMBING PROJECT

Select a challenging route with the goal of sending it.

CLIMBING SECTOR

Sectors are areas within a climbing area or crag, composed of a set of routes.

CLIMBING SHOES

Special shoes used for climbing, lightweight and with grippy soles.

CLIPPING, TO CLIP

Refers to the act of placing the rope through the carabiner of the quickdraw, which will be hanging on a fixed bolt.

DHARANA

Concentration, directing the attention to a single point.

DHARMA

Own path, duty, natural law, vocation, purpose of life.

DHYANA

Meditation, deep and prolonged concentration.

EQUANIMITY

Balance of the mind, imperturbability.

FREE CLIMBING

Climbing using only one's own skills, without the aid of materials to progress in the ascent. The only equipment used is for protection in case of a fall (such as rope, harness, belays and fixed anchors on the wall).

HATHA YOGA

Yoga consisting mainly of physical practices such as asana or pranayama.

ISVARAPRANIDHANA

Surrender to the higher.

JNANA YOGA

Yoga of spiritual knowledge, of learning.

KARMA

Means "action" and is interpreted as the consequence of actions. Cause and effect.

KARMA YOGA

Yoga of action, dedicating one's actions to the higher.

NIYAMA

Disciplines for self-refinement, moral purification.

ON-SIGHT CLIMBING

Sending a route without having tried it before or having received information about it.

PATANJALI
Author of the Yoga Sutras

PRANAYAMA
Regulation of breath and energy.

PRATYAHARA
Control/withdrawal of the senses.

QUICKDRAW
Two carabiners joined by a sewn sling that are used to attach the rope to the fixed anchors of the route, hooking one carabiner to the plates of the route and passing the climber's rope through the other.

RAJA YOGA
Yoga of the mind, it is the one described in the Yoga Sutras of Patanjali.

ROUTE
A climbing route is the path a climber uses to climb a wall. Sport climbing routes are usually equipped with fixed anchors that allow the safety rope to be placed along the ascent. They can have different shapes and characteristics and are graded based on their difficulty.

SADHAKA
Person who practices a sadhana.

Sadhana

Path toward spiritual growth.

Samadhi

Higher state of absorption or total integration, realization; consequence of meditation.

Samyama

Application of dharana, dhyana and samadhi towards something.

Sanskrit

Ancient Indo-European language in which most of the sacred texts of India are written.

Santosha

Contentment.

Satya

Truth, sincerity, honesty in thought, word and action.

Saucha

Cleansing, internal and external purity.

Sending, to send

Climbing a route (leading) from start to top without falling or using artificial anchors to rest or progress. The anchors and other protection material are only used as a safety measure, but not to facilitate progression.

Sport climbing

Climbing modality understood more as a sport practice that consists of climbing walls of different difficulties equipped with fixed anchors placed to protect the climber's safety.

Sutra

Axiom, aphorism that condenses the essence of a knowledge with the minimum amount of words.

Svadhyaya

Study of the scriptures and of oneself.

Tapas

Discipline, perseverance.

Top rope climbing

Climbing with the rope already mounted on a top anchor so that the rope is always above the climber. It is the safest way, ideal for beginners.

Viveka

Intellective discrimination, discernment.

Yama

Moral and ethical codes of yoga.

Yoga

Physical, mental and spiritual discipline that aims to still the mind and reduce its fluctuations.

Yoga Sutras

One of the most influential texts of Yoga, it constitutes a synthesis of the various beliefs and practices of yoga.

Yogic Readings

Yoga Sutras, Patanjali
Bhagavad Gita

Recommended translations and commentaries on Yoga Sutras

The Yoga Sutras of Patanjali, Sri Swami Satchidananda
Light on the Yoga Sutras, B. K. S. Iyengar
The Yoga-Sûtra of Patañjali, Chip Hartranft

Recommended translations and commentaries on Bhavagad Gita

The Bhagavad Gita, translation by Juan Mascaró
The Living Gita, a commentary for modern readers by Sri Swami Satchidananda

Book Series
Wisdom from the Rock

Stoic Climbing.
Finding Wisdom on the Rock

Climbing and Tao.
The Way of the Route

Climbing is the New Yoga

Keep working on your climbing *sadhana* with us. Subscribe to our mail list!

climbingletters.com/mail

Made in the USA
Monee, IL
12 December 2023